Creative Initiative

Creative Initiative

Guide To Fulfillment

To Dale Bidenbaugh
for One Earth, One
Humanity and One Spirit
Harry J. Rathbun

Harry J. Rathbun

Creative Initiative Foundation
Palo Alto, California
1976

Library of Congress Cataloging in Publication Data

Rathbun, Harry J.
Creative Initiative

Includes Appendices and Suggested Readings
I. Philosophy.
ISBN 76-485-69

Printed in the United States of America

Albert Einstein: *The World As I See It* by Albert Einstein, © Estate of Albert Einstein.

Loren Eiseley: *The Night Country* by Loren Eiseley, © 1971 Loren Eiseley. Reprinted by permission of Charles Scribner's Sons.

Viktor E. Frankl: *Man's Search For Meaning* by Viktor E. Frankl, published by Beacon Press.

Else Frenkel-Brunswik: "Meaning of Psychoanalytic Concepts and Confirmation of Psychoanalytic Theories" by Else Frenkel-Brunswik, *Scientific Monthly.* Volume 79, pp. 293–300, November 1974.

Erich Fromm: From *Man For Himself* by Erich Fromm. © 1947, © 1975 by Erich Fromm. Reprinted by permission of Holt, Rinehart and Winston, Publishers. *The Art Of Loving* by Erich Fromm, published by Harper & Row, Publishers, Inc.

George Gallup: *The Miracle Ahead* by George Gallup, published by Harper & Row, Publishers, Inc.

William Glasser M.D.: *Reality Therapy: A New Approach To Psychiatry* by William Glasser M. D., published by Harper & Row, Publishers, Inc.

Hermann Hagedorn: "The Bomb That Fell On America" by Hermann Hagedorn, Association Press, New York. © Hermann Hagedorn Estate.

Edith Hamilton: *The Greek Way* by Edith Hamilton. © 1930, 1943 by W. W. Norton & Company, Inc. © renewed 1958, 1971.

Learned Hand: "Mr. Justice Cardozo" by Learned Hand. Reprinted by permission of The Yale Law Journal Company and Fred B. Rothman & Company from *The Yale Law Journal, Columbia Law Review,* and *Harvard Law Review.*

George Russell Harrison: *What Man May Be* by George Russell Harrison, published by William Morrow & Co., Inc. © 1953 by The Atlantic Monthly Company, Boston, Mass. Reprinted with permission.

The Harvard Committee: "General Education in a Free Society" by The Harvard Committee, published by Harvard University Press in 1945.

Gerald Heard: *The Eternal Gospel* by Gerald Heard. © 1974 by Jay Michael Barrie. *Training For The Life Of The Spirit* by Gerald Heard. © 1975 by Jay Michael Barrie.

William Ernest Hocking: "The Atom as Moral Dictator" by William Ernest Hocking, published in the *Saturday Review.*

Aldous Huxley: From pp. 260, 2–4 in *Ends And Means* by Aldous Huxley. © 1937 by Aldous Huxley. Reprinted by permission of Harper & Row, Publishers, Inc.

William James: *The Varieties Of Religious Experience* by William James, published originally by Longman Green.

Rufus Jones: *A Call To What Is Vital* by Rufus Jones. © 1950 Macmillan Publishing Co., Inc.

Elizabeth Parkhill Jordan: "Dominion" by Elizabeth Parkhill Jordan, *Scientific Monthly,* Vol. 60, February 1945. p. 116.

Søren Kierkegaard: *Works Of Love* by Søren Kierkegaard, published by Harper & Row, Publishers, Inc.

Thomson King: "Atomic Power" by Thomson King, *Scientific Monthly,* Vol. 63, October 1946. p. 248.

Rudyard Kipling: "If" from *Rudyard Kipling's Verse,* Inclusive Edition by Rudyard Kipling. © 1910 by Rudyard Kipling. Reprinted by permission of the Estate of Mrs. George Bambridge and Doubleday & Co., Inc.

Walter Lippmann: *A Preface To Morals* by Walter Lippmann. © 1929 by Walter Lippmann. Renewed 1957 by Walter Lippmann.

Oswald W. S. McCall: From pp. 122–123 in *The Hand Of God,* Enl. Edition, by Oswald W. S. McCall. © 1939, 1957 by Harper & Row, Publishers, Inc. Reprinted by permission of Harper & Row, Publishers, Inc.

Abraham Maslow: From *Toward A Psychology Of Being* by Abraham Maslow. © 1962 by Litton Educational Publishing, Inc. Reprinted by permission of D. Van Nostrand Company. *Motivation And Personality* by Abraham Maslow, published by Harper & Row, Publishers, Inc.

William C. Menninger M.D.: "The Criteria of Emotional Maturity" by William C. Menninger M.D., published by The Menninger Foundation.

Ashley Montagu: *On Being Human* by Ashley Montagu, published by Henry Schuman, Inc.

Herbert J. Muller: *The Uses Of The Past* by Herbert J. Muller, published by Oxford University Press.

Max C. Otto: *Science And The Moral Life* by Max C. Otto, published by New American Library, Inc.

William L. Pelz M.D.: "Adolescence in the Age of Longing" by William L. Pelz M.D. © Friends Publishing Corporation. Reprinted from *Friends Journal.*

Theodore Roszak: From *Where The Wasteland Ends,* © 1972 by Theodore Roszak. Reprinted by permission of Doubleday & Co., Inc.

Max Schoen: *The Man Jesus Was* by Max Schoen. © 1950 by Alfred A. Knopf, Inc.

William Sheldon, Ph.D., M.D.: *Psychology And The Promethean Will* by William Sheldon, published by Harper Brothers, 1936.

Pitrim A. Sorokin: *The Ways And Power Of Love* by Pitrim A. Sorokin, published by Beacon Press.

G. N. M. Tyrell: *The Nature of Human Personality* by G. N. M. Tyrell, published by George Allen & Unwin Ltd.

Gregory Vlastos: *The Religious Way* by Gregory Vlastos, published by Women's Press.

Robert Penn Warren: "Brother to Dragons" by Robert Penn Warren, published by Random House, Inc.

Leroy Waterman: *Religion Faces The World Crisis* by Leroy Waterman, published by George Wahr Publishing Co.

Lancelot Law Whyte: *The Next Development In Man* by Lancelot Law Whyte, published by Holt, Rinehart and Winston, Inc.

Henry Nelson Wieman and Walter M. Horton: *The Growth Of Religion* by Henry Nelson Wieman and Walter M. Horton, published by Harper & Row, Publishers, Inc.

George Will: "Run For Your Life" by George Will. © 1976 by Newsweek, Inc. All rights reserved. Reprinted by permission.

Dedicated to God, The Most High,
to all who have received
the Golden Thread of the enlightened life,
and to all the brotherhood
who live in the spirit and by the truth.

CONTENTS

FOREWORD

This book is written for people who feel deeply the need for a rational, solid, workable basis for their lives. If you are one of those people, this book is for you. The principles set forth here are universal. They are the product of many people's experience, and they have proven practical and rewarding for those who have lived by them.

The entire philosophy presented here is eclectic. By that we mean that it comes from many different sources. It includes whatever we have found both true and relevant, wherever it comes from. The test for truth is experience. The test for relevance is that any particular truth, to be included, must contribute to a rational, meaningful, satisfying way of life.

The effort has been to make the flow of thought and feeling simple, direct and readily understandable. To achieve that in this particular subject is not easy. Nor is it easy for anyone to put into effective action the principles which yield the greatest meaning and fulfillment in one's life. No one can do it for anyone else. But you can do it for yourself, and the effort is richly rewarding.

There are statements in the book which may seem to you dogmatic or authoritarian, even arrogant. When a statement evokes such a feeling, we ask you to remember two things: (1) There is an obvious difference between what is authoritarian and what is authoritative; (2) One who makes a *tentative* statement is *unsure* of its truth, is motivated by a false humility, or is being strategic. The strategy may be either to avoid an appearance of arrogant dogmatism, or to suggest a thought for the reader to weigh and make an independent judgment. There is nothing tentative, authoritarian, or arrogant about saying dogmatically, "Two plus two equals four." But the statement can properly be called authoritative because it is *known* to be true.

We have sought to support many of the statements made in the book with sound and logical reasons. Others, made without such substantiation, have seemed to be self-evident, either at once or after careful pondering. The entire presentation should prove to be internally consistent and make sense to the penetrating mind. The intention is to share with you discoveries which have been made by workers in this most important area of mankind's thought and action.

Throughout the book there occurs a constant refrain: "The test for truth is experience." When that test is met, the predicted results follow in a cause-and-effect relationship. If the principles presented here do not meet that rigorous test, they should certainly not be believed, much less acted upon!

The process with which this book deals is the "hero's journey" found in the wisdom myths of all peoples. This is the life journey which every human being has to take. For a successful outcome it is crucial that the correct guideposts be followed. The pages that follow present those guideposts.

Since this book deals with the human condition, we shall be using interchangeably such terms as "mankind," "the human being," "homo sapiens," and "man". It is an unfortunate limitation of our language that the word "man" has two meanings, the *human being* and the *male* of the species. We shall use the word *man* in the generic sense except where we distinguish between the male and the female. Then we shall use the words man *and* woman. We shall have to use the pronouns "he," "his," "him" in the generic sense also. All of this is to say what we have to say in the least awkward way.

This book has come into being through the cooperative effort of many people. It would be impossible to identify all who have contributed and to give proper credit for what they have given. Indeed the original intention was for complete anonymity, but two names must be mentioned. The graphic design of the book and the illustrations are the work of Mike Lee. Typography and production were under the direction of Bob Holmes. We are deeply grateful to both for their contribution.

INTRODUCTION

THE GOAL

What do you really want most for your life? If you are hungry, certainly you want food. If you are cold, you want warmth and shelter. These are basic needs. But when people's basic needs are met, they are not content. A desire for something more is a driving force built into the very nature of mankind. In this, the human being differs from all his animal relatives. For the animal, life runs through a cycle: birth, foraging for food, reproduction and death. But that won't do for man. He yearns for something more deeply satisfying. He wants his life to have *meaning*. Yet his efforts to find it, even though propelled by a powerful built-in drive, generally fail to be fulfilled. Why?

Basically, it is because he doesn't know *what* it is that gives meaning to life. Consequently, he could not know how to go about achieving it. People proceed by trial and error, repeating the same mistakes generation after generation. They pursue a whole range of short-term goals which they believe will yield meaning. These include such things as pleasure, sensation, excitement, money, possessions, popularity, power. The pursuit of any or all of these goals, even when achieved, leads inevitably to the realization that none of them satisfies the inborn demand for meaning. Only the wisest and most perceptive people have discovered where the error lies and how to correct it. Fortunately their findings are available to us, and that gives us hope. This book is designed to help you understand what some of the wisest human beings have discovered. Then you can decide whether you want to follow their instructions to find true meaning and fulfillment for *your* life.

Four things need to be said here:

First: The route by which meaning is achieved is an individual process. Like breathing, or eating and digesting your food, no one but you can do it. This is a personal journey for every individual.

Second: Once the map, the guideposts, and instructions for the journey have been laid out, the decision to embark is entirely your own.

Third: The principles involved and the directions for using them do not call for your accepting anything on "blind faith." They are profound but simple, and can be rationally perceived and understood. Truth, after

all, can be tested. The test is experience. The question to be asked is whether the stated cause-and-effect relationship works out as predicted.

Fourth: There are two familiar routes for experiencing truth, and we must integrate both. These are the *mental,* and the *feeling-emotional* capacities of the human being. In this book, of necessity, the principles and concepts involved are set forth in "intellectual" terms. These are the terms with which the mind deals. But even when one's mind has grasped a concept, one's feelings may not immediately agree. Have you not had the experience: "I *think this,* but I *feel that*"? For these two ways of perception to be brought together in agreement, an additional discipline is involved. It is called *meditation.* One aspect of this discipline involves pondering what has been perceived at the mental level, turning it over and over in the mind, looking at it from all possible angles and levels, until not only is the mind satisfied as to its truth, but the feelings have come to agree. When this union of mind and feelings occurs, there is a gratifying sense of certainty and of standing on solid ground.

This unifying discipline is very important. When the mental and the feeling-emotional components of a person are pointed in opposite directions, their powers cancel each other out. But when both are lined up in the same direction they add up to personal power. This unification is necessary for *personal integration.* When the mind and feelings are in agreement, power is released for action.

THE BASIC QUESTIONS

A basic conclusion follows from what has been said. Our problem is *ignorance.* People generally do not achieve *meaning* in their lives because they *don't know* what will really satisfy their desire for something more significant than life has thus far given them. It has already been pointed out that, since we do not know what it is that gives our lives meaning, most people spend theirs in exploring blind alleys. Our most important question, therefore, is: "What must I *do* to achieve meaning for my life?" It is the purpose of this book to answer that question.

There are two preliminary questions we must answer first: "What is the nature of man and what is his destiny?" "What is the nature of the world in which we find ourselves and in which we must function?" These questions will be explored in the chapters that follow, but there are important hurdles which we must first clear. These hurdles exist because all three of these are religious questions, and the words "religion" and "religious" present barriers for many modern minds. So let us face the problem honestly and dispose of it. Several elements are involved:

THE CLOSED MIND. The quest for truth in any area calls for an open, objective, unprejudiced mind. This is the attitude of detachment which is the essence of the scientific spirit. The scientific endeavor is the search for *truth,* in whatever area is under examination. It is clear that in such a search, matters of opinion are obstacles to discovery, because people are attached to their opinions. Bias, prejudice and attachment to particular outcomes are fatal impediments to the discovery of objective truth.

SUPERSTITION. The religious quest and religious activity have always dealt with the problems of man's survival and well-being in a world full of mysteries, and real or imagined threats. People's earliest religious expressions therefore dealt with what they believed they had to do to appease any possible or imagined sources of those threats. These expressions involved theories or models of the way people thought the world operated. These were models of what they believed to be reality, of the way things are. In developing these models, people imagined a variety of gods and demons to explain things they did not understand. The inevitable result was that in mankind's early history, religions were primitive, childish, superstitious and filled with magic and mystery.

RIGID HIERARCHIES. It was also inevitable that a priestly class should develop, people who specialized in this area, and that the concepts, models, and practices should become institutionalized and rigid. Institutions and their rigidities tend to persist. That tendency has resulted in the continuation, even to our own time, of much in the area of religious creeds and practices which the modern sophisticated, scientifically-oriented mind cannot accept. This constitutes a major crisis in credulity.

HYPOCRISY. People have been turned away from what they believed to be the religious aspect of life by their experience with people who professed, or were reputed, to be religious but whose lives did not manifest a quality it seemed desirable to emulate.

The experience of many people has been to encounter these difficulties. As a result, they have rejected the whole religious enterprise as they have perceived it. If you are among those who, for whatever reason, find the words "religion" and "religious" repugnant, consider the following:

(1) The words are derived from the Latin *religio, religare,* to tie or bind together, or to bind *back* (*re* plus the same root from which comes the word *ligament*). The idea here is related to that which is represented by the psychological term, *integration.* Religion, therefore, properly deals not only with man's survival, but also with the integration or wholeness of the human personality, and meaning for his life.

(2) Meaningful survival, therefore, is the goal of the religious enterprise (as it is also of the psychological enterprise). For that, there is no necessity for it to remain in a primitive, superstitious, or outmoded state. It can be as sophisticated and realistic as science, as indeed it must be if modern man is to pay any attention to its teaching.

(3) Everyone has some set of values, ideals, concepts and ideas about reality, about the way things are. These he holds consciously or unconsciously—undoubtedly some of both. He also has ideas about what he has to do for his own survival and well-being. The sum total of all of these ingredients makes up his *philosophy of life,* his religion. It follows that everyone of us has a religion, whether we are aware of that fact or not. By that collection of concepts, ideas, ideals and values, we make all our decisions, although we are largely unconscious of the part these various elements play in the process. When we come to realize that, we are forced to conclude that our religion is the most important thing about us! That means that it had best

be a good one. A "good one" is sophisticated rather than primitive, mature rather than childish, founded on reality rather than on illusion, and must in no way be in conflict with the discoveries of science.

(4) When we say that we are dealing with religious questions, we are pointing out that we cannot avoid using religious language. For the free flow of thought, it is therefore necessary that we drop any prejudices or negative associations which such language may carry for us.

(5) Many of the perceptive people of history who have understood the basis of meaning, integration and life-fulfillment have been religious geniuses. We shall have occasion to examine some of their findings. The process to which you are being introduced by this book is eclectic in that it incorporates relevant truth wherever found. We say again that experience is the test for truth. But to be incorporated in this process, any particular truth must also meet the test of relevance to the goal. The goal is fulfillment of our inborn destiny, the realization of our potential, the achievement of meaning for our lives.

THE PLAN OF THE BOOK

In writing this book, the effort has been to present the underlying philosophy and the resultant practical process as simply as possible and to have the presentation flow smoothly in a logical sequence. A variety of ways of explaining concepts and principles can often be helpful. To avoid interrupting the basic outline, supplementary material is presented in appendices at the end of the book. Appendix A relates to this introduction and contains statements on the general subject of religion from a variety of sources. These can be helpful by way of enrichment and perspective.

Questions and exercises occur frequently throughout the book. These are designed to assist in the process of assimilation and integration. We urge you to meditate upon them and to write both your thoughts and your feelings. The text is directed to your mental process. The questions and exercises, in conjunction with meditation, are designed to help you bring your

feeling-emotional functions into the process. We suggest that you write freely, in a journal or in the margins of this book—notes for future pondering and evaluation.

While this process is a personal undertaking for every individual, help, joy and satisfaction can be had by working in company with others. This can provide the additional assistance of sharing and checking out discoveries with companions on the journey. If you can get a small group of people to join you on this project, meeting regularly to share and discuss findings, your progress and theirs can be greatly accelerated.

Questions and Exercises for Meditation

1. What has been your personal experience in Sunday School? in churchgoing? in religious education in home and school?
2. How do you feel about these experiences?
3. What religious creeds, dogmas, doctrines, theology and practices have you been unable to accept, and why?
4. What are your feelings about all these elements?
5. What has been your experience with so-called religious people?
6. Can you distinguish what you *think* from how you feel about them?
7. What additional reactions do you have to the idea that the quest for meaning for your life is a religious enterprise?
8. To what extent does what we have said about the true nature and subject matter of religious activity help remove your own mental and emotional blocks to the use of religious words?
9. Do you still have such blocks?
10. How willing are you to remove them?
11. What positive experiences have you had in the religious area?

CHAPTER I

What is Man?

THE BASIC QUESTION

What is man, that thou art mindful of him? and the son of man, that thou visitest him? For thou hast made him a little lower than the angels, and hast crowned him with glory and honour.

Psalm 8: 4, 5

If I am to realize the greatest possible meaning for my life, I must know what I have to work with. The matter of first importance, therefore, is to know what is the nature and what is the destiny of mankind in general, and of myself in particular. What am I? Who am I? Where am I in the life process, and where am I going? What is my built-in potential? What can I *be* at my highest and best? What choices are open to me?

Aristotle's comment is helpful: "The true nature of anything is the highest it can become." By that standard, the true nature of man is what he can be at his highest and best. That is what we want to know when we ask about the nature and destiny of man. We can approach the answer from four different directions. These are the approaches of history, science, art, and religion.

In the historical approach, we look at the way we arrived at our present state of evolution. By seeing where we have been, we can tell something about where we are going.

The sciences of anthropology, sociology, and psychology have insights to contribute. What do they tell us? The artist has a different way of looking at things. It could be called a "feeling" way. The poets and other artists in the use of language can express their insights in ways that have a double impact on consciousness. Language used artistically has both mental and emotional impact.

We said that the questions we are asking are religious. We should therefore expect to get important insights from the religious geniuses. What do they see as man's potential, his goal and destiny? What can man be at his highest?

THE APPROACH OF HISTORY

Here, we inquire into the route by which we have arrived at our present stage of development. What is the direction of mankind's curve of advance? By extrapolation—by extending that curve into the future—we can derive a sense of where we are going, of what is our destiny.

Let's take a brief look at our evolutionary history. It is a very long story, which began about two billion years ago. The first life on this planet was most probably a single living cell, our first ancestor. In the evolutionary story of life on this earth, many organisms developed and became extinct along the way. But the line in which man evolved tells an amazing success story. It is hopeful for our future to realize that during all of those two billion years none of our ancestors died or became extinct until they had reproduced their kind.

There are several outstanding features in that long story. These are significant in tracing the direction of our past line of advance and projecting what lies ahead if we continue the process.

First. Our beginning was in water, our first home.

Second. Development moved from a single cell through continuously increasing numbers of cooperating cells in more and more complex groupings.

Third. Reproduction at first was by simple cell division, but at some point became bisexual.

Fourth. The move from the sea to the land went through an amphibian stage.

Fifth. Evolution into the mammalian form was an important advance.

Sixth. Movement of the quadruped to the upright stance of a biped was extremely significant. It freed the forepaws to develop into hands, those highly useful and sensitive instruments of curiosity and investigation. With the four fingers and opposable thumb of his hand, man has developed remarkable skills. These have been of immeasurable usefulness in acquiring knowledge about his world.

Seventh. The crowning development was that of the computer housed above the ears, the human brain. This endowed us with the powers of reason, of reflec-

tion, of consciousness of the individual as an identity. It gave us an aesthetic appreciation, a sense of time—past, present, and future—that is unique among our fellow creatures, and an increasing capacity to perceive reality.

The paleontologist, Pierre Teilhard de Chardin, has summarized the direction of the human advance in two terms, *complexification* and the development of *consciousness*. The complexification process involved moving from a single-celled blob of protoplasm to a multi-billion-celled human being. In man all the billions of cells have specialized functions. All perform fantastically in a highly complex and organized cooperative system.

A striking feature of the evolutionary process is that every human being, during the first nine months of his life, recapitulates most of that two-billion-years-long story of his biological evolution. The individual's life begins as a fertilized human ovum. It continues by evolving in a bag of water and nine months later the multi-billion-celled human infant emerges from the womb into a new environment.

We can make deductions from this human evolutionary story which are significant and challenging. In answer to the question about the nature of mankind, one crucial thing we can say is that as a result of his development of consciousness the human being is equipped with an inherent capacity to perceive reality. Perception of reality is what we mean by *consciousness.* By the word *reality* we include not only "the way things are" as apprehended through the senses; we include also their cause-and-effect relationships. The reality with which we are concerned further involves not only the total of the surroundings within which we live, but also our own nature, our potential, and our destiny. It must be clear that the more accurately we perceive reality, the more wisely we can act for our own well-being and for the well-being of the whole system to which we belong. Accurate perception of reality puts us in position to answer the three basic questions which are the subject matter of this book. To restate them, these are:

1. What am I?

2. What is the nature of the environment in which I must function?
3. What must I do for meaningful survival?

Questions and Exercises for Meditation

1. Consider the success story that lies in your past if it is true that your living cells started with that first "blob of protoplasm."
   Do you feel you have realized your potential? At the end of your life would you like to be able to say "yes"?
2. How would realizing your potential help your children and the human race?
3. What in your experience has moved you to reach for fuller consciousness?

THE APPROACH OF SCIENCE

The process of science is to discover and formulate the functioning relationships in any specific area under investigation. The key word is *discover*. Science deals with reality. And by reality we mean "the way things are." Instead of "functioning relationships" we more commonly speak of "cause and effect", but either way we are talking about the same thing.

Science rests on the basic faith that we live in an orderly universe. It holds that there are dependable relationships in the structure of reality. It holds further that these can be discovered by patient, honest, detached investigation. Such investigation involves the formulation and testing of hypotheses. Each hypothesis is based on a theory, formulated by the scientist, as to what he thinks may possibly be the relationships under study. The hypothesis is then tested in the laboratory to find out whether it matches the reality. If it does, we say that a scientific law—a law of nature—has been discovered. Science is the process of reducing mystery to knowledge.

In the science of psychology the subject matter is the human psyche. It deals with the operation of the mind, emotions, feelings and spirit of man. Because of the intangible nature of the subject, the testing of hypotheses is more difficult than in many other areas of scientific investigation. But psychologists are continuously accumulating dependable knowledge about the human psyche. It is an interesting and encouraging fact that by the careful, painstaking, and objective procedures of science, psychologists are gradually verifying insights which have long been understood by religious geniuses. The same observation can be made about insights of researchers in anthropology and sociology. These two branches of humanistic science, dealing with the evolution of man and with his relationships, must also be included in assessing what the approach of science has to contribute to our understanding of the nature and destiny of mankind.

It is relevant here to point out that there are four ways of knowing, four routes by which knowledge reaches our conscious awareness.

The first of these is the *physical.* Input comes through the five physical senses: seeing, hearing, touching, smelling, and tasting. These are tremendously aided by the vast collection of technological instruments created by man. In the matter of seeing, for example, we have eye glasses, binoculars, two-hundred-inch telescopes, microscopes, electron microscopes, radio telescopes, television, the printed page, and the whole range of photography and other graphic arts. Then there are all the supplementary devices by which information is made available to the eye by meters, dials, graphs, charts, and computer print-outs. Through instruments like these all the various physical stimuli are focused, amplified, intensified and recorded for intake into our consciousness. We are so accustomed to the use of all these technological aids to our perception that it is easy to forget how much we depend on them.

The second route is the *mental*. This reasoning faculty for analysis, reflection, deduction and synthesis works with the physical data collected. It deduces, extrapolates, generalizes, and formulates hypotheses on various aspects of reality to be tested and either verified or refuted. It also proliferates and invents more instrumentation to collect and process more and more of the physical data.

The third route is through the *emotional-feeling-aesthetic* faculties. This area is more difficult to define precisely but we have seen that it is very important to take into account. For example, to see beauty, one must recognize aesthetic relationships. Otherwise one can be in the presence of beauty and not know it. This route is more advanced than the mental and is the avenue through which we approach the highest level of knowing.

The fourth level is that of the *spiritual,* the intuitive, the way of direct cognition. It is to this plane that we must move. Here the great break-throughs of human perception have occurred, whether in science, art, music, or religion. It is in this, the field of direct perception of reality, that people have their communication with Ultimate Reality, with God. That is the level of knowledge, wisdom, purpose, consciousness—by whatever name we choose to call it—which exists above and beyond us and to which we are subject. The experience of a direct relationship with *that* is what constitutes religious experience. This involves recognition of the fact that there is a plane of consciousness and intention as much above the human as the human is above those of plants and animals. Just as plants and animals are subject to human will on this earth, the human being is subject to this higher plane of authority. Later chapters will deal more fully with this important subject.

We return now to the findings of the humanistic sciences on the basic question: "What is the nature of man?" We know the difficulty of testing hypotheses in this area of science. That testing has to be accomplished by finding out how the projected principles actually work in people's lives. That takes time and extensive observation. It follows that many promising hypotheses have been developed which are not yet established as *law*.

There is a growing body of psychological hypotheses which fall within this category. Some of the contemporary pioneers in the field are willing to speak with conviction about their conclusions while, at the same time, pointing out that full verification by the slow, painstaking procedures of science has yet to be achieved.

It will be sufficient here to summarize briefly some relevant conclusions from the humanistic sciences. A sampling of significant statements by individual workers in this area will be found in Appendix B. The human being is seen by them to have the inborn capacity for mental health. It is his destiny to be healthy in body, mind and spirit. The manifestations of mental ill-health—variously called neurosis, psychosis, schizophrenia, paranoia, insanity, etc.—are aberrations.

The mentally healthy human being manifests detachment, realistic perception, responsibility, courage, and love for his fellow man and for the world, his home.

THE APPROACH OF AESTHETICS

The ancient Greeks recognized the trilogy of *truth, beauty,* and *goodness* as the supreme values. The artist's devotion is to beauty and his work deals with aesthetic perception and appreciation. He has ways of communicating aspects of reality through media which appeal to the corresponding faculties of the viewer. Painting, sculpture, architecture, music and literature communicate different aspects.

In this book we are concerned first of all with truth regarding the nature and destiny of the human being. In this section we seek the insight of the artist in the field of literature. The artist with words has a special facility for communicating aspects of truth in a way which can make a double impact by reaching both the mental and the feeling-emotional levels at the same time. In his poem, *If*, Rudyard Kipling sets forth qualities which make for wholeness and maturity in the human being.

If you can keep your head when all about you
  Are losing theirs and blaming it on you;
If you can trust yourself when all men doubt you,
  But make allowance for their doubting too:
If you can wait and not be tired by waiting,
  Or, being lied about, don't deal in lies,
Or being hated don't give way to hating,
  And yet don't look too good, nor talk too wise;

If you can dream—and not make dreams your master;
  If you can think—and not make thoughts your aim,
If you can meet with Triumph and Disaster
  And treat those two imposters just the same:
If you can bear to hear the truth you've spoken
  Twisted by knaves to make a trap for fools,
Or watch the things you gave your life to, broken,
  And stoop and build 'em up with worn-out tools;

If you can make one heap of all your winnings
  And risk it on one turn of pitch-and-toss,
And lose, and start again at your beginnings,
  And never breathe a word about your loss;
If you can force your heart and nerve and sinew
  To serve your turn long after they are gone,
And so hold on when there is nothing in you
  Except the Will which says to them: "Hold on!"

If you can talk with crowds and keep your virtue,
  Or walk with Kings—nor lose the common touch,
If neither foes nor loving friends can hurt you,
  If all men count with you, but none too much;
If you can fill the unforgiving minute
  With sixty seconds' worth of distance run,
Yours is the Earth and everything that's in it,
  And—which is more—you'll be a Man, my son!

The literary form of poetry reaches both the mind and the emotions. Prose can also achieve this as the following excerpt demonstrates:

" 'His name shall be in their foreheads,' said the Book. 'They shall see His face and His name shall be in their foreheads. They become like that which they loved,' said the Book. Then I fell to dreaming and the spirit spoke to me until I knew not whether to shudder or rejoice.

"Be under no illusion, you shall gather to yourself the images you love. As you go, the shapes, the lights, the shadows of the things you have preferred will come to you, yes, inveterately, inevitably as bees to their hive. And there in your mind and spirit they will leave with you their distilled essence, sweet as honey or bitter as gall, and you will grow unto their likeness because their nature will be in you.

"As men see the color in the wave so shall men see in you the thing you have loved most.

"Out of your eyes will look the spirit you have chosen.

"In your smile and in your frown the years will speak.

"You will not walk nor stand nor sit, nor will your hand move, but you will confess the one you serve, and upon your forehead will be written his name as by a revealing pen.

"Cleverness may select skillful words to cast a veil about you, and circumspection may never sleep, yet will you not be hid. No.

"As year adds to year, that face of yours, which once, like an unwritten page, lay smooth in your baby crib, will take to itself lines, and still more lines, as the parchment of an old historian who jealously sets down all the story. And there, more deep than acids etch the steel, will grow the inscribed narrative of your mental habits, the emotions of your heart, your sense of conscience, your response to duty, what you think of your God and of your fellow men and of yourself. It will all be there. For men become like that which they love, and the name thereof is written on their brows.

"There is one revelation of you which must be made. *MUST*."

Oswald W. S. McCall
"The Hand of God"

Questions and Exercises for Meditation

1. Did you like Kipling's poem? McCall's prose? To what extent does your mind have to consent before the feelings are experienced?

2. Which moved you more—Kipling or McCall? With which did you mentally make a connection?

3. What qualities would you list as identifying the mature person?

4. What do people see written on your face?

THE SPIRITUAL-INTUITIVE APPROACH

The fourth way of knowing is that by which "break-throughs" occur, not only in religious insights but also in both art and science. It has been called "integral" as distinguished from "analytical" thought.

The religious geniuses, like geniuses in other areas, have had better access than the ordinary human being to this fourth level of knowing. Their perception of truth is penetrating and precise. At this point we will use but a single example. This is from what has been called "The Sermon on the Mount". It occurred in the setting in which Jesus of Nazareth was pointing out how his teaching goes beyond mere obedience to the formal law.

> "Ye have heard that it was said, Thou shalt love thy neighbor, and hate thine enemy: but I say unto you, Love your enemies, do good to them that hate you, bless them that curse you, pray for them that despitefully use you.
>
> "If ye love them that love you, what thank have ye? for even sinners love those that love them. And if ye do good to them that do good to you, what thank have ye? for even sinners do the same.
>
> "Ye shall be sons of the Most High; for he is kind toward the unthankful and evil: he maketh his sun to rise on the evil and the good, and sendeth rain on the just and the unjust. Be ye merciful, even as your Father is merciful."

Jesus suggests that mankind's destiny is to become "sons of the Most High." For this highest possibility of the human being to be a reality a total process must be undergone. That process is what this book is all about.

Questions and Exercises for Meditation

1. "Son of the Most High" stands for a person's highest achievement. What does it mean?
2. What would a city or town be like if everyone were working at being their "highest"?
3. What would keep a person from going for the "highest"? What about you?

THE TOTAL HUMAN ORGANISM

One further thing needs to be said about the nature and destiny of man. This is most important, but generally we are only vaguely conscious of the complete inter-relatedness and interdependence of all the functions in every human being. These include not only the highly complex organic systems of the physical body, but also the mental, emotional, aesthetic, intuitive and spiritual functions.

We have some primitive awareness of this interdependence when we talk about psycho-somatic illnesses. But the importance of deep understanding of these relationships is generally unrecognized.

Think of just the complex operations of the various systems of our physical bodies and how they are totally inter-connected and dependent on one another. Think of the fantastic cooperation among the billions of cells which make up these systems. And think how they function smoothly without our conscious awareness, in spite of all the ignorant and stupid things we do to interfere! It inspires awe to meditate on the intricacy of our physical endowment.

We need to realize how important is the cooperation of all systems, not only of our physique but also of our psyche, for the realization of our highest and best state of knowing and being. Achievement of that state is our destiny as human beings. It is the built-in goal for our lives. But its realization depends upon our conscious and informed choice to follow the correct path toward its realization.

Questions and Exercises for Meditation

1. Ponder deeply on how your mind, your emotions, your motivation, and your will power are affected by your physical health, and vice versa.
2. What is physical pain? What is psychological pain?
3. How can you deal with your psychological pain?

IN SUMMARY

The conclusions we draw from the foregoing material can be summarized in four statements:

1. The human being possesses a capacity to perceive reality and is in an evolutionary process of increasing consciousness.
2. Our destiny is to continue that process with ever more accurate *knowledge* of reality and resultant *action*, for the well-being of the whole system of creation of which each of us is an inextricable part.
3. Fulfillment of that destiny is to have identity, to be truly *Homo Sapiens*, and to be involved in a dynamic living process which yields deep meaning to life.
4. That identity is manifested in qualities of clear perception, responsibility, dependability, generosity, and love for all mankind and for the planet.

CHAPTER II

Our World

THE CHALLENGE

We have been considering what a remarkably complex organism the human being is. The world in which man emerged was also a vastly complex totality. All of its widely varying parts were in dynamic balance of interdependency. Each fulfilled its particular function in relation to the whole, just as do the individual cells and organs of the human body.

But we humans, in our ignorant arrogance, have drastically interfered with the balance of nature. We have made the world uninhabitable for some living species and are now in grave danger of making it so for all life, including our own. That human arrogance is the product of ignorance. Ignorance is the root of all evils.

It is obvious that we have misunderstood an ancient insight contained in the creation myth as it is set forth in the biblical book of Genesis. According to that story, when man was created he was given dominion over all the earth. The basic insight was that man was to be the responsible caretaker of the planet. The misunderstanding lay in man's assumption that the world was his property to exploit as he might choose. We have done this, with results which are now catastrophic. We are at the crisis point where we must make a drastic change in our total outlook and our actions. If we fail to do that, mankind has a very short and disastrous future. There is reason to hope that there is still enough time. But it seems clear that there is little more than just enough.

The crisis in which we find ourselves has many aspects. It is not the purpose of this book to discuss these in any detail. Much has been written about them and is available. Appendix C lists some of the problems which must be solved if mankind is to survive on this earth. It also suggests some introductory reading for those who might require further evidence that we are on a disaster course.

All of this is part of the answer to the second basic question with which we must deal: What is the nature of the world in which we find ourselves? The material in Appendix C deals with the negative side of the question. It is important, however, to take account of the positive aspects also.

THE HOPE

Despite the frightening nature and the enormity of the world-wide crisis, this is no time for despair. There are reasons for hope, but hope based on realities, not on wishful thinking.

First of all, there is a growing awareness of our predicament. To see a problem clearly is the first necessary step toward its solution. This awareness has led to an increasing and widespread dissatisfaction with things as they are. The positive result of this is a broad reaching out for something better. Because the reality of our dilemma can be so frightening when clearly seen, some of the reaction can only be labeled as sheer escapism. This is a very common human reaction, but it is not the only response being made. Some of the outreach is a search for deeper personal meaning and significance. Some of it recognizes the need for fuller consciousness. Some is a responsible search for relevant answers. These are constructive directions. They set an atmosphere conducive to correcting the ignorance which produced our dilemma.

Dispelling ignorance is the task to be accomplished. And that is an educational undertaking. Education (from the Latin *educare, to lead out*) is a process of helping people toward clear perception of truth. *Truth,* like its companion word, *reality,* means *the way it is.*

There are available solutions to our problems. The great persons of history, the seers, the prophets, the saints, the wise ones who have appeared from time to time, have something significant to say to us. They have been in fundamental agreement on what is the basic human need, what is the proper goal for mankind, and how we must proceed to achieve its realization. They had insight into our basic questions: the nature and destiny of man, the nature of his total environment, and what man has to do. Our educational job is to make known what the wise ones knew and how to apply that knowledge to our problems.

We have stated that the process of fulfilling our human destiny is a religious activity. One of the aspects of the religious impulse is to share one's insights with others. Because of the permanent effect of some of man's actions on nature, such as the release of radioactivity, destruction of the ozone layer of the atmosphere, and exhaustion of irreplaceable natural resources, this has become a life-or-death matter.

Two of the seers of the past who are recognized to be among the greatest of the religious geniuses were Gautama, called the Buddha, and Jesus of Nazareth. In both cases, after achieving enlightenment—after attaining mature perception of reality—they sought to share their wisdom and experience by teaching what they had discovered. With Gautama this was summarized in *the eightfold path;* with Jesus, in the *Sermon on the Mount.* In a very dangerous situation for his people, Jesus saw the necessity to challenge a set of narrow, short-sighted, but stubbornly-held suicidal positions. These, he knew, would lead to the destruction of the national life of his people if not radically altered. He was not successful in bringing about the necessary change in attitude by the people who controlled the situation. The outcome which he foresaw followed within forty years. But his unwavering course, of seeking to dispel a fatal ignorance, led inevitably to his early death. In this instance, as in many others, history has shown that truth is not always welcomed by those who have taken rigid contrary positions.

Religion has been defined as "a passion for righteousness and for the spread of righteousness, conceived of as a cosmic demand." That statement is worthy of careful thought. The term *cosmic demand* implies a necessity which is written into the very structure of reality. The word *passion* denotes a deep and moving emotional conviction. *Righteousness* means doing what is right. The *spread* of righteousness means sharing the necessary knowledge with others so they can know what they must do to achieve fulfillment of their potential. That is the sense of *mission* which has motivated all the great religious geniuses.

This ingredient of the religious impulse should be seen as crucial to the solution of our problems today. This is emphasized further by the fact that, although a genius makes important independent discoveries on his own, most people have to be *taught.* That fact places on the person who "knows", a special obligation to share any truth which is important for the survival and well-being of the human race. Privilege imposes

responsibility. Ignorance generates the need to be taught.

Questions and Exercises for Meditation

1. What are your thoughts and feelings after considering the threats to our life and well-being listed in Appendix C?
2. To what extent do you presently feel some concern for awakening others to the dangers that threaten us?

THREE DIMENSIONS: SPACE, TIME, LIFE

In considering the nature of our world, there are three elemental and mysterious factors that we need to ponder. These are *space, time,* and *life.*

All material objects, including ourselves, occupy *space.* To gain perspective on this factor, it is helpful to imagine what it would be like to move out away from the earth, and to continue forever, without coming to an end of space. If that takes you beyond your power of imagination, try the alternative. Imagine that your journey into outer space does bring you to the end of space. When you try those two exercises of the imagination, don't you get a clear feeling that there are great mysteries beyond your power of understanding?

Then ponder *time.* We are all subject to time. Its unrelenting march carries us along with continuous change from birth to death. Change is one thing about time of which we can be certain. As with space, can you imagine either a beginning or an end of time? When we speak of *time,* what really are we talking about? What *is* time? Can you explain it? Although we live "in time" how often do we stop ("take time") to wonder about it? Another mystery.

Life is a marvelous, complex and mysterious phenomenon. It is the fact on which our very existence rests, but we take it for granted without much effort to get our bearings within it or ponder its meaning.

Meditation upon these three dimensions of our environment evokes a consciousness of awe and wonder, of mystery, of humility. The same feeling is evoked by meditating upon the marvelously intricate, intelligent, cooperating system of the human body. Deeply pondering these mysteries leads to a realization that we are in the presence of something vastly greater than ourselves. Something was here and functioning long before we arrived on the scene. We are forced to an appropriate humility when we come to realize that there are great and inescapable mysteries about existence which we have not been able to fathom, but to which we are totally subject.

LIFE—DEATH GOOD—EVIL

The world we live in constantly confronts us with choices between opposites *Life and Death, Good and Evil.* Two other names for the opposites, *Good* and *Evil,* are *Right* and *Wrong.* Good or Right is that which makes for the continuation of life and the evolutionary process toward greater and deeper consciousness. Whatever is contrary to that process is Wrong or Evil.

It should be pointed out that there are those who contend that good and evil, right and wrong, are only relative terms. These people are correct to the extent that these terms are relative to whatever *goal* is involved. They are mistaken, however, when they go on to claim that there is no objective standard for what is right or wrong. Once the goal is established, it is clear that there *is* an objective test for what leads to that goal. For man, the goal is a dynamic process of continuing evolution toward wider, deeper, and fuller consciousness and an accurate perception of reality.

Further evolution for man is not automatic, not a matter of chance, nor is it preordained. Man must consciously choose it. Whether man achieves fulfillment is a matter of conscious decision. It is a matter of extreme importance that this be clearly understood. The sobering reality is that if we do not decide, with conscious and whole-hearted intention, to continue our psychological and spiritual evolution, our level of consciousness deteriorates. It has been said, "He who is not getting better is getting worse." The crucial question is whether we choose to move forward, or whether by inaction, by failure to make the crucial choice, we allow ourselves to drift toward despair and ultimate disaster. It is a matter of life versus death, fulfillment versus frustration, triumph versus failure. Being born into this life, with the great heritage of mankind's evolutionary past, has bestowed upon each of us a great challenge and exciting opportunity. Historically, this is the time of a crucial choice. Of the two outcomes, Shakespeare has written:

> There is a tide in the affairs of men,
> Which, taken at the flood, leads on to fortune;
> Omitted, all the voyage of their life
> Is bound in shallows and in miseries.
> . . . . . .
> We must take the current when it serves,
> Or lose our ventures.

WHAT IS REALITY?

Another way of stating the second of man's three basic questions is, "What is reality?" What is it that we have to perceive, if we are to work successfully within the framework of reality? There are three aspects to this subject which need to be understood:

First. By the term *reality* we are speaking of "the way things are", or "how it is". That's what we mean when we talk about *objective reality.* We mean the opposite of illusion or falsity. We are inseparable parts of the entire system of reality. We are within it; we cannot secede or escape from it. Whatever affects it affects us, and whatever affects us affects it. Whatever we do, or neglect to do, has its impact on all the future down to the end of time. When we see that, the implication of man's having dominion over all the earth places upon us a profound responsibility from which we cannot escape.

Second. We must perceive the realities of the situation in which we find ourselves at any moment with as much clarity and accuracy as possible. It is essential that we see it as it actually is.

Third. We have seen that man has dominion over the earth. But we have also seen that he is completely subject to reality, which is *the way it is.* What, then,

happens to our freedom? The answer is that we have none; we are completely subject to *the way it is, the way things are.* At any given moment there is absolutely nothing we can do about that, other than to *accept* the fact. There is something we can do about the way it *will be,* but nothing about how it *was* in the past, or as it *is* in this moment. When it is put that way, it seems so obvious as not to be worth saying. Yet it is necessary to say, because it is so generally disregarded. When we are faced with a particularly difficult situation, we tend to say, "Oh no! It can't be!" Or, "I can't take it!" Or more commonly, "It shouldn't be." Recognizing our unwillingness or reluctance to face and accept the reality is the first step. The essential attitude is *acceptance* of the reality. It is the starting point for wherever we are going, and whatever we are going to do. Acceptance does not mean contentment or satisfaction with things as they are. Neither does it mean resistance to, or rebellion against, reality. It does mean completely recognizing the fact that things are as they are. Resistance to the reality, rebellion against things as they are, get us nothing but frustration. In any situation where we find ourselves, we can make only a *second* move; the first has always been made before we get there. However, we can take initiative for the *second* move. But it will be *creative* initiative only if we accept the reality, and if we have previously undergone the self-discipline necessary for meeting the demands of the situation. It is this creative second move that takes us out of any situation, out of the way things *existentially* are, into a *better,* life-serving situation.

Questions and Exercises for Meditation

1. Think back over some situations in which you have resisted or rebelled against reality, and the results.
2. Think of some when you responded with acceptance.
3. How do you feel about those situations and their outcome?
4. What will make it possible for you to take creative initiative in future situations?

STRUCTURE

Another general observation about reality is important for our understanding. Everything in the universe has "structure". The structure of anything is "how it is", "the way it is", its *"is-ness"* at the moment. It is a way of talking about *specific* aspects of reality, which we shall discuss later in more detail. To say that everything has structure seems again a redundant statement, so obvious as to be foolish. But notice how it relates to what we have just been saying about *acceptance.* It is essential to see clearly what actually, *at the moment,* is the structure of anything with which we have to relate.

The qualifying phrase, "at the moment", suggests that the structure of whatever we are talking about may be subject to change. That is indeed true of most things. Their structures do change over a span of time, but at greatly varying rates. The structure of a rock on a hillside changes slowly. But the structure of the mixture of gas and oxygen in a cylinder in the motor of an automobile changes very rapidly when ignited by a spark from the spark plug. The structure of a mind-set can change in an instant, or it can remain locked, as though frozen in time.

There is, however, a type of structure which, *if* it changes at all, does so at such an exceedingly slow rate that it may be treated as unchangeable, for all practical purposes. That type of structure is what we call "natural law", a "law of nature", or "scientific law". A scientific law is a formulation of relationships which we regard as completely dependable and therefore unchanging. The philosophy of science is based on the faith that, in our universe, there is this immutable or unchangeable *dependability* of certain relationships. The purpose of science is to discover and formulate accurate statements of these relationships. We talk of "cause and effect", but it seems to the scientist more precise to speak of "definition of relationships".

In the realm of mathematics, physics, and chemistry, common-place illustrations are such as: $2 + 2 = 4$; $e = mc^2$; $2H_2 + 0_2 = 2H_2O$. We unquestioningly treat these formulations of relationships as dependable and therefore unchanging. All branches of science have their own sets of laws.

One branch of knowledge, not yet fully accepted into the family of sciences, is that of psychology. But the whole basis for psychology as a science, is the faith that there are "laws" in this more elusive field of man's psychological development and relationships. The effort of psychology is to discover these dependable relationships.

Questions and Exercises for Meditation

1. Would you accept the outcomes of love and hate as being dependent upon psychological "laws"?
2. What psychological "laws" would you list as dependable and unchanging?
3. Would you be willing to obey these laws?

AUTHORITY

When we look at the evolutionary story of man and his development of consciousness, we are led to the important conclusion that there is a great intention and purpose behind all creation. We conclude that the universe is friendly to the development of consciousness, because that development is rewarded. It is part of a vast system. Developing consciousness pays dividends to those who achieve it and keep moving in the process of its continuous deepening and expansion. This realization leads to a totally objective basis for dealing with *good* and *evil*. Again, good is that which contributes to the development of consciousness; evil is whatever works against it. Good is what makes for the *meaningful survival* which was dealt with in the Introduction.

Our observations, our pondering and our experience all lead inescapably to a conviction that there is a will, a purpose, greater than our own which governs the whole system of which we are parts. We are subject to it and must be conscious of it. We have to be obedient to it if we are to achieve the realization of full meaning for our lives. Its conditions must be met if we are to fulfill the destiny which is written into the very structure of the universe. This is the essence of religious consciousness. In religious language the will

greater than our own is called "the will of God". The whole religious enterprise for any individual is to *do* the will of God. That is to do what is *right,* that which is *the highest,* that which yields the greatest good for all.

Religious consciousness is the awareness that there is a spiritual reality underlying the phenomenal world. This is the supreme and ultimate reality we call God. Once man comprehends this he realizes that there is purpose, intention and direction in Creation. It is alignment with this which gives the human being meaning for his life. You who read this may well have ruled out or ignored this crucial fact for understandable and logical reasons. As we have said, these have probably been based either on your observation of hypocrisy and poor performance in professedly religious people, or on *the unreasonable demands on your credulity* made by some of the institutional expressions of religion you have encountered. Or it may be that the general concept, which we have just introduced, has never been forcibly brought into your consciousness. Whatever the reason, the crucial necessity, at this point, is to keep your mind open, hold to the basic scientific spirit of honest inquiry and investigation of the relevant evidence, and then see how far you can honestly, and with full integrity, go toward acceptance of what has been said. If you cannot yet accept all the statements made above, we ask that you refrain from rejecting them until you have read further, and weighed carefully what you read.

What has been said up to this point has dealt almost wholly with man's spiritual and psychological evolution. But man's psyche is housed in a physical body, and the two are presently inseparable. Hence we cannot ignore the fact that our very physical survival is under the most severe and widespread threats man has ever encountered. It is therefore necessary that we take full account of the critical nature of our predicament.

It is equally necessary that we be fully open to the discovery that there are available to us *powers* greater than our own, that there is an *intention* in the vast scheme of things, and that the "noble experiment" of man on Planet Earth need not end in disaster. It is clear, however, that the outcome rests upon the decision of man himself. In the vast scheme of creation the choice has been given to us. Hermann Hagedorn, in his epic poem, *The Bomb That Fell On America,* has put it well:

> "Man without God is a bubble in the sea, a single grain of sand on an infinite beach.
> God without man is a mind without tongue or ears or eyes or fingers or feet.
> God and man together. We are such power as not all the atoms in all Creation can match!"

IN SUMMARY

We stand today at a turning point in mankind's history. We have to make a conscious choice, of an all-encompassing magnitude never before faced by man. If we choose to move on the right path, we can have a bright future. But if we do not make that right choice, our future is bleak, dark, and short.

The trouble we are in has been caused by ourselves—by people. The 24 threats to our existence listed in Appendix C are all people-caused. And they have to be remedied by people—by you and me. If we do not act to correct the situation, who will? The government? The politicians? Big business? Small business? The church? The university? The school? God?

If your religious faith leads you to believe that God is going to intervene miraculously in human history, to save man from the inevitable consequences of his stupidity, from the operation of cause and effect—of natural law, you are not going to find comfort in this book. For although this book is based on a deep religious faith, that faith is not one based on magic, or superstition, or the setting aside by a capricious God of the natural law established by the creation of the universe we inhabit—however and in whatever specific manner that creation took place. History shows that the working of God on this planet among men is *through* men, who are willing to be the media for that work. Man has been given the power of that choice. That means that man can prevent the fulfillment of

God's purpose if he does not choose to aid it! That is a sobering thought, the impact of which man has not yet fully grasped.

Questions and Exercises for Meditation

Write on your thoughts and feelings about:

a. a Will greater than our own;
b. a level of knowledge higher than our own, to which we may gain direct access through the trained intuitive capacity;
c. your destiny as a human being;
d. the crisis of our planet;
e. realistic hope for man's future on this earth;
f. the partnership of God (Creator) and man (co-creator).

CHAPTER III

The Self: Essential & Existential

THE HUMAN SITUATION

We have been saying that the inborn human potential points to a high destiny for every person. That destiny is to be enlightened, and that means to be perceptive, mature, responsive, harmless, cooperative, loving, socially responsible. How many people like that do you know? Why are they so rare?

We said that ignorance is the basic obstacle to that achievement. Ignorance of our true destiny allows us to follow wrong paths that lead away from fulfillment rather than toward it. But if man is made for a high destiny, and if the way to its realization has been discovered, taught, and demonstrated by the wise ones of history, why does ignorance persist?

THE DETOUR

The answer has several aspects. The evolution of consciousness, of awareness, of true perception, is a long slow process. The civilizing venture, which depends on consciousness, must therefore also be long and slow. It began in *unconsciousness,* in ignorance, and the deepest ignorance is unawareness of the fact of the existent unconsciousness. But that is precisely the place where we began. We need to remind ourselves that our evolutionary history is not only long, but that it began at ground zero. The development of consciousness from savagery toward civilization called for a steep and arduous climb out of the pit of ignorance. History records a succession of rare individuals who broke through the barriers of the primeval ignorance, and rose to high levels of civilization, of maturity, illumination and fulfillment. They pointed the way to reach that level, but the crowd has lagged far behind.

Our present state of ignorance and crisis is not a *fall* from some higher, ideal human state. It is rather a crisis point on the journey where we have encountered a great obstacle to further progress. That obstacle is so large that it will mark the end of our journey, unless we choose to surmount it.

Surmounting this obstacle will mean overcoming the ever-present reluctance of the many to follow the teaching and example of the perceptive few. It will also require facing the fact that we have taken a detour from the true path to fulfillment. The nature of the detour is indicated by Items 1, 2 and 13 on the list of threats to our survival in Appendix C.

1. The mounting rate of violent crime—murder, rape, armed robbery, etc.

2. The frightening growth in terrorism throughout the world.

13. The breakdown of moral, ethical and spiritual values resulting in such outcomes as the break-up of the family as a basic social institution, the aberrational exploitation of sexual expressions, juvenile delinquency, drug abuse, alcoholism, pornography.

For items 1 and 2, surely one important contributing factor is the tremendous development of technology. That has provided incredibly destructive tools to those who engage in criminal action and international warfare. Another cause for these two threats is stated in Item 13, but what led to that breakdown?

The basic cause seems to be a misreading of a signpost on the way to fulfillment and the consequent departure from the correct route. Consider the following chain of events. The last hundred years have brought a rapidly increasing interest in human psychology. One of the causes of this concern may well have been the rapid developments in technology and in the whole social and economic structure which these have brought about. These have assuredly produced psychological tensions, pressures and maladjustments. Whatever the causes were, the revolutionary contributions to psychological knowledge and thought made by Freud and other pioneers have resulted in the emergence of many theories and schools of thought in psychology, psychotherapy and psychoanalysis. These range through a wide spectrum between two contrasting extremes. At the risk of undue over-simplification and generalization, we suggest the following rough description of these.

At one end of the spectrum is the position that much psychological distress is caused by conscious and unconscious feelings of guilt resulting from failure to measure up to certain moral and ethical standards. These standards were regarded by those who developed this position as unrealistic and as having their source in codes of conduct variously called *Victorian, puritan, religious, Christian,* etc., and, in any event, regarded as not grounded in reality. It followed logically that guilt could be eliminated and psychological well-being restored by removing the pressure to conform to these illusory standards. That, of course, required the perception that they were in fact illusory. In this general school of thought, some have claimed that the terms "right and wrong" and "good and evil" are purely subjective, having no objective reality.

The opposing view holds that the ethical ideals criticized were developed out of human experience in the civilizing process of mankind, and that they have proven to be generally sound and of personal and social utility. The resulting position in this veiw, then, is that the psychological pressures, repressions and neuroses caused by guilt can be alleviated, not by changing or doing away with the ethical standards, but by helping individuals discover how to raise their level of maturity, responsibility and conduct. By that accomplishment, the guilt-producing gap between performance and standards would be bridged.

In evaluating these two contrasting positions, we would have to say that the first calls for less personal and social responsibility. It would obviously be more attractive and popular among people reluctant to increase the area and depth of their responsibility. We observed that such reluctance is widespread and natural. Nothing else is to be reasonably expected unless the individual person can see that there is value and benefit in accepting increased responsibility. In the absence of such perception, the misreading of the guidepost and the resulting departure from course could hardly have been avoided.

We have sought to show that there is an objective base for what is right. The criterion for judgment is whether the attitude and action being weighed contributes toward or moves away from the growth of consciousness, and the consequent personal and social responsibility, of the persons involved.

It must be obvious that the position taken in this book is aligned with the second view rather than the first. That position is based on the insights, teaching and experience of religious geniuses, the thinking and experience of contemporary workers in psychology and related social sciences, and our own observations and experience. From those who have actually traveled the route, we have trustworthy guideposts, map and directions for our journey. That fact, and the growing awareness of the seriousness of our dilemma and of the necessity to get back on the path of advance, all give hope for the future. The work we have to do is arduous, but the reward will be worth all it requires.

Questions and Exercises for Meditation

1. Ponder deeply the chaos brought about by "Item 13."
2. Study carefully the material in Appendix B. Based on your own observations of reality what makes "good" sense to you?
3. Consider the other threats listed in Appendix C and see whether there are others that you regard as more basically important.

THE ESSENTIAL SELF

We have seen that the marks of mental health are wholeness, clear perception of reality, the resolution of inner conflict, creativeness, courage, generosity, love. These are the characteristics spontaneously manifested by the person whose living is directed from his true center, from his soul, his conscience, his essential self, the ground of his being. All of these terms will be used interchangeably because they speak about the same thing. This will become increasingly apparent as our discussion progresses. Such a person is manifesting his true potential. He is "self-actualizing", and is in a dynamic process of self-realization, of the fulfillment of his destiny, of achieving the goal of his life. This is

not a goal of some kind of imagined perfection, but is a *state of being* in which there is a dynamic, perceptive, responsive and creative relationship with reality.

In contrast to the few people in human history who have achieved such a level of being, most people have operated, not from their true center, but from the frame of reference which throughout this book we shall call the *existential self*. We have already indicated that in using the contrasting term, *essential self,* we are speaking of the released inborn capacity of every human being for correct perception.

THE EXISTENTIAL SELF

The existential self, as its name suggests, is the *existing* frame of reference from which people operate until they succeed in releasing their essential self to take command. It is important to understand how the existential self functions, if we hope to remove it from its controlling position, and to enthrone instead the essential self.

The *existential* self is the overlay, the egocentric shell, which imprisons the essential self and thus prevents its proper functioning. The existential self does this by blocking, diverting, screening, and distorting the input of data coming from the environment. The effect of this is to prevent a person from seeing things objectively—as they really are. The *existential person* has a frame of reference, a point of view, from which he looks at everything. His existential self consists of a set of prejudices, preconceptions, expectations, ideas, ideals, standards, "should's," and "should not's" from his past. These come from the conditioning to which he has been subjected by his environment. The existential self therefore sees things subjectively instead of objectively. Subjectivity means that things are seen not as they really are, but as "processed" through all the layers of the individual's conditioning. As a consequence, the resultant actions, based as they are on an incorrect, distorted and incomplete view of the realities, are egocentric, unrealistic, unwise. They lead away from self-realization, not toward it.

We are generally aware that the egocentric person is motivated by such negative forces as greed, fear, inner conflict, illusion, ignorance, pride, prejudice, hostility, revenge, violence, hatred, frustration. His manifestations, in varying proportions and intensities, are given such names as neurosis, psychosis, schizophrenia, catatonia, insanity, or merely selfishness, ill-temperedness, ineffectiveness. Glasser (Appendix B) lumps these all together under one term, "irresponsibility".

If the true center, the true essence, of man is a perceptive capacity, a *conscience* (con = "with"; science = "knowing")—the discriminating capacity to know *right* from *wrong,* why should this aberrational perception and behavior take over? What we have been saying is that this behavior is a result of *conditioned reactions.* We shall need to consider how the conditioning occurred, how it operated to create the existential self, how that imprisons the *essential* self, and how we can rescue and release the true self to fulfill its proper function.

THE EFFECT OF OUR CONDITIONING

Since the existential self is a conditioned self, what we *are,* at any given moment, is a complex psychophysical structure made up of three components: (1) the endowment we were born with; (2) what our environment has done to that; and (3) what we have done with those two ingredients. The last two items comprise our conditioning.

We are provided with three basic drives which we may think of as instinctual. These are the survival or "self-protective" drive, the procreative or "sex" drive, and the drive toward meaning and fulfillment. We have the first two of these in common with all our animal relatives. The third is peculiarly human, pushing us in the direction of the development of consciousness. It is the "divine discontent", the drive to evolve further. The first two drives have to do primarily with aspects of our physical needs, but more and more they become psychological as well. Man is a psychological as much as a physical entity. The self-protective drive

now causes us to put up defenses not only against threats to life and physical well-being, but also against what we regard as threats to our psychological well-being. If someone attacks, derides or ridicules an *idea* we hold, we feel that *we* have been attacked, because we have become identified with that idea. Our defense mechanisms are immediately marshalled to swing into protective action.

THE TWO SELVES IN OPERATION

It will be helpful to consider at some length how the functioning of the two selves differs. The essential self operates from the base of *detachment* and the effort to be objective. It is not attached to any idea, prejudice, hypothesis or point of view. It is attached only to the *abstract ultimate values of truth, beauty, and goodness.* It is detached from all else. It was an important insight of the ancient Greeks to recognize truth, beauty and goodness as the highest values. The *essential* self perceives reality freed from the distorting, screening and diverting influences of the layers of conditioning to which all of us have been subjected.

The *existential* self, on the other hand, is still subject to all those influences. Its perceptions, therefore, are incomplete, inaccurate, distorted. The actions based on such perceptions must consequently be inadequate responses. Inadequate perception necessarily leads to inadequate action. The conditioning to which we have been subjected has provided each of us with a particular frame of reference. From this individual perspective we view all the information and data coming into our range of observation. The result is a distorted picture of reality registered in our consciousness. What we think to be real, objective, and the way things are, is not the way they really are at all.

There are differing degrees of seriousness in the phenomenon of inaccurate perception. The more flagrant manifestations of the distortion of reality are called *insanity.* We label others as "out of touch with reality", or neurotic, psychotic, or paranoid. However, there are many familiar lesser manifestations. In these it is still obvious to any critical observer that the

person is not seeing things as they really are. We then say that he is biased or prejudiced. By that we mean that he operates from a frame of reference or point of view which disenables him to see the actuality of the particular situation. We are acutely aware how difficult it is to get such a prejudiced person to change his frame of reference and thus to discover the relevant realities.

Since few of us realize how completely conditioned we are, we do not consciously set about the process of de-conditioning ourselves. We view everything from our own individual frames of reference, believing that we are seeing reality. New ideas which shake our established frames are disturbing and uncomfortable. Therefore we tend either to reject them outright, or at least to resist shifting our frame.

Viewing everything from one's own frame is called *egocentricity*. That word refers to the situation in which one looks at the whole world from oneself as the center of reference. We say that in this situation one is self-centered, or self-involved, or selfish. The opposite position is that of objectivity. In that position the viewer sees things as they actually are. The result of true objectivity is *acceptance,* which is the only attitude from which positive progress can be made toward the release of the *essential* self.

SOURCES OF OUR CONDITIONING

The *conditioned* self is another term for the existential self, which *exists* in the unenlightened person, the person who has not achieved wholeness, self-realization, self-fulfillment. Among the most important conditioning factors which produce this existential self are the experiences of very early childhood. These include the trauma of birth and the negative experiences of having one's early dependent needs ignored or inadequately met. They involve experiences such as the feelings of abandonment, rejection, ridicule, depreciation—all the innumerable experiences which cause psychological injuries. These experiences evoke the survival and defense mechanisms which the child needs to survive those injuries. All of this collective experience becomes

part of a person's conditioning, most of it repressed into unconsciousness or subconsciousness.

These survival and defense mechanisms generally cause the child who is endowed with an aggressive temperament to fight back or rebel. If the native temperament is passive, the reaction is generally to capitulate or withdraw. In either case the psychological survival mechanism tends to cause repression of the feelings of hurt into the unconscious mind, and thus to block them out of memory, because they are unbearable. This repression has two consequences. The first is to make the hurt feelings inaccessible to conscious memory, precisely because they are so painful. The second consequence is that unconscious energy has to be expended in keeping the feelings continuously repressed, for the same reason.

When the repressed feelings can be brought to consciousness and properly handled, energy is released for more creative purposes. The particular limitations caused by the conditioning can then be transcended, and effectiveness in living greatly enhanced.

For most people, the early relationship with one's mother is the most important area of early conditioning. That relationship, or one with a mother substitute, begins as a state of total dependency. It is a most intimate relationship in which the child is exceedingly vulnerable. Such relationships are never perfect so they are never free from some negative factors; inadequacies can be extraordinarily traumatic. The relationship with one's father is generally next in importance.

Other obvious factors in one's conditioning are the rules—or the lack of them—spoken or unspoken, of the household in which one grows up. Others are relationships with brothers or sisters, with teachers, with peers, and other important people in one's life. Add to these jobs held and social groups one has belonged to. All of this experience has contributed to forming the existential self, the current *structure* of one's mind and emotional life.

The variations among people, in the depth of their access to the recollection and reliving of childhood hurts, suggest a wide range of approaches to the task of deconditioning. For the most difficult situations, pro-

fessional psychological assistance may be required. But for many, a disciplined intentional commitment to the necessary change in one's patterns of conscious intention and action will be sufficient to get the process under way. Persistent, disciplined practice of responsible *conduct* produces change in a person's *character*. This, in turn, leads to the deepening of *consciousness*. The sequence of steps in the process can be succinctly formulated in the three words: *conduct, character, consciousness*.

Questions and Exercises for Meditation

1. Ponder the implications for you of being totally conditioned.
2. In what areas of your personality are you the most defended and protected? Why?
3. What is the most vulnerable relationship in your life? How does your conditioning affect it?

THE PRINCIPLE OF DETACHMENT

Contemporary man has been led to worship uncritically at the throne of Science. He has tended to overlook the most basic requirement of the truly scientific spirit. That requirement is a total commitment to *truth in the abstract,* coupled with detachment from everything else.

In order to enunciate the principle of detachment it seems almost inevitable that we resort to statements that appear paradoxical. It is indeed the principle enunciated more than nineteen centuries ago by Jesus of Nazareth in what is known as "the great paradox". Its simplest form occurs in the Gospel of Luke. In the familiar King James Version of 1611 the translation reads: "Whosoever shall seek to save his life shall lose it; and whosoever shall lose his life shall preserve it." A marginal note in the English Revised Version of 1881 gives "*soul*" as an alternative translation for the word "life". This really seems more accurate because the word is "psyche" in the Greek, the language in which the book was written. One New Testament scholar has asserted that none of the familiar English translations does justice to the powerful words of the original Greek. He has suggested that a free translation, giving those words their full impact, would state the principle thus: "He who seeks to preserve his psyche by building around it thick walls of protection and defense will utterly destroy it; but he who destroys all such walls and defenses will free his psyche to emerge as a living, vital thing." It is clear that two different *psyches* or *selves* are being talked about, and that the effort to preserve the "existential self" will result in the failure to set free the "essential self", the true psyche.

An analogy which fits the situation is that of the unhatched chick in its shell. Before hatching, the chick's life is preserved by the shell. Without this protection the chick would perish. But when the time for hatching comes, unless the chick expends the considerable effort to break out of the shell and discard it, the result will be death by strangulation within the shell.

During the earliest years of life, a natural process has built up around the essential self a protective shell of defense against the hurts to which it is inevitably subjected in an imperfect world. Nature seems to provide for the human being the survival mechanism of this protective psychological shell, just as it provides the chick with its life-protecting shell. In those early years this seems actually necessary for the young child's very survival. But, as in the case of the chick and the egg shell, a time comes when the protective shell becomes a death-trap. Then it must be discarded if the life-process toward fulfillment is to continue. Otherwise the egocentric shell persists as a life-defeating neurosis.

The life-fulfilling process has been spoken of symbolically as death and rebirth, as crucifixion and resurrection. Those strong words are aptly used because the process involves drastic psychological surgery. But every individual, like the chick in the shell, has to perform this operation for himself. It calls for creative action initiated from within. No one else can do it for him. Every human being, however, can and must do it if he is to fulfill his destiny, free his essential being, achieve enlightenment and become fully human. This truth cannot be too strongly emphasized. It is indeed a life-and-death matter.

Two contemporary renderings of the principle are helpful in giving additional perspective. The American poet, Robert Penn Warren, in *Brother to Dragons* puts it this way:

> "The recognition of the direction of fulfillment
> is the death of the self,
> And the death of the self is the beginning of selfhood."

The contemporary Austrian psychiatrist, Viktor Frankl, says this:

> ". . . the real aim of human existence cannot be found in what is called self-actualization. Human existence is essentially self-transcendence rather than self-actualization. Self-actualization is not a possible aim at all, for the simple reason that the more a man would strive for it, the more he would miss it. For only to the extent to which man commits himself to the fulfillment of his life's meaning, to this extent he also actualizes himself. In other words, self-actualization cannot be attained if it is made an end in itself, but only as a side effect of self-transcendence."

Questions and Exercises for Meditation

1. Try writing about your understanding of the principle of detachment and your feelings about it. Write on how far you have been able to bring your reason and your feelings into agreement on this.
2. Do the same on the subject of the "great paradox".
3. How do you respond mentally and emotionally to the death-and-rebirth concept? Think and write about those responses.
4. From what do you need to detach?

CHAPTER IV

The Human Life Process

THE SEVEN FACTORS

The basic question that concerns us is what we have to do to realize our highest potential and fulfill our destiny as human beings. In seeking the answer we need first to know the nature of the life process to which we are subject and within which we work. It is through that process that we either fulfill our destiny of self-realization, or end up in disappointment and frustration. The result depends on our making the right choices at the decision points. Like any other natural process, this one is subject to dependable cause-and-effect laws of relationship that are as binding as those of any other aspect of natural law. It is very important to understand what these laws are.

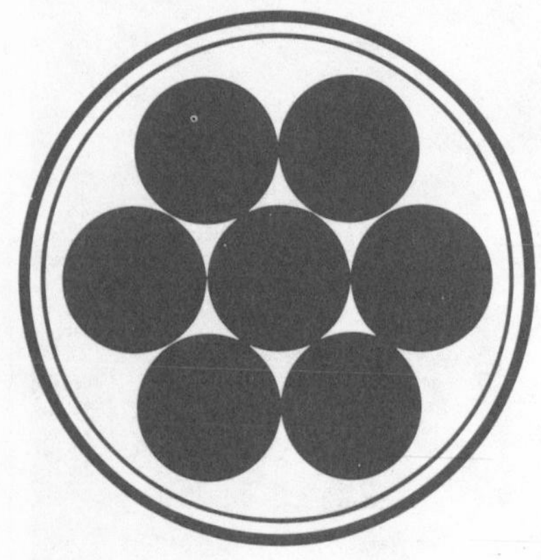

Analysis of the human life process reveals a system which can be set forth in seven elements. We will designate these by the descriptive terms: *structure, function, need, dialogue, method, nature,* and *social outcome.* The first three, *structure, function, need,* are the "givens". These are the factors we begin with; they are the realities we have to work with in any situation we face. The next two, *dialogue* and *method,* deal with the action to be taken. They tell us what we have to do about the givens. The last two, *nature* and *social outcome,* are the results, personal and global, of what we do. The aspects of dialogue and method are directly involved in answering our basic question.

STRUCTURE FUNCTION AND NEED

We stated earlier that everything in the universe has *structure.* This is simply a way of affirming the obvious: namely, that everything is the way it *is.* Why do we have to labor that obvious fact? Again, it is because of the *inescapable necessity* that we see things as they actually are. We must know the data with which we have to work and the principles that govern. But we have seen that there are many obstacles in the way of perception and understanding. The fact is that our view is generally distorted and incomplete. If we are to act wisely we must have accurate perception. So the first necessary step is understanding with the mind how the process operates.

A simple mechanical analogy will make clear the basic interrelationship among the three givens. Take the example of an electric fan. Its *structure* determines its function. That is what it was designed to *do*. The *function*, which is the purpose of a fan, is to move air. In order to perform that function an electric fan has a *need* to be plugged into a source of electricity. Choose any illustration of mechanical tools or instruments, and observe how these three aspects are interrelated and interdependent. The structure of each determines its function, but in order to fulfill that function it has needs that have to be met. The engineer who designed the particular mechanism began with the desired function and worked back to develop an appropriate structure which would perform that function. Function requires structure. Structure determines function. But every mechanism requires some kind of input in order to fulfill its function. That is its *need*.

Moving from purely mechanical illustrations we can see that with living things the same relationships exist among the givens. The function of an acorn, determined by its structure, is to produce an oak tree. Its needs are soil, moisture, heat, and light from the sun. Its total structure is such that it can become an oak tree if those needs are met.

In plants and animals the life process is a circular or cyclical one. With animals it involves birth (or some form of beginning of the individual life), growth to maturity, reproduction, generally some nurturing of progeny, and finally death, with the return of the physical remains into the continuing life processes of the planet.

With the human being, the development of consciousness has enabled the life process to become less circular and more linear. It is intended to *go* somewhere other than just around a circle. The basic relationships among the givens continue to apply, but because of mankind's complexity it is less easy to see just how they operate.

For the human being the process can lead in either of two directions. It can move toward self-realization, wholeness, and life-fulfillment, or toward frustration, defeat and despair. We said that the direction it takes for any person depends on a crucial decision that he, himself, has to make. It is a decision that must be made consciously, with knowledge and understanding of what one is about, if the direction is to be toward self-fulfillment. The continuance of our psychological evolution is up to us; the choice is ours. If we understand how the process works, we can make the correct decisions, which are those that lead to fulfillment. If we do not know what we must do, and we therefore fail to make the proper choices, the inevitable negative outcomes follow.

Any perceptive observer sees innumerable examples of the failure to make right choices. One of the religious geniuses proclaimed that the way to fulfillment is narrow and difficult, and added, "Few be they that find it." It is no longer necessary that they be few. The essential knowledge is available to those who are open to see.

THE RIGHT HUMAN FUNCTION

In the healthy human being all his cells, organs, and systems correctly perform their individual functions in cooperation with all the others. By that cooperation each part is enabled to perform its specific function because it is provided with whatever it needs in order to do so. It is a total system of complete interconnectedness and interdependence of all the parts. It involves their unlimited cooperation for the well-being and proper functioning of the whole.

In the larger system of our world, the same interdependence of all the parts exists. There is also the same necessity for the cooperative functioning of every individual unit. Every human being is an individual social unit, an inextricable part of the whole system.

In the evolutionary process man has been developing consciousness. Consciousness is accurate perception. Wider and deeper consciousness means better awareness of reality. The more accurate one's perception, the greater the wisdom of one's actions, both for one's own well-being and the well-being of the whole system. In man's development of consciousness, self-consciousness was a step. By that he became aware of a power of choice. The human being can decide whether to comply with the conditions for his continued development, or to rebel. Unfortunately for his own well-being and that of the whole world, his ignorance of ultimate consequences has led him, for the most part, to make the wrong choice.

Today we are experiencing the emergence of a new level of awareness of the interdependence of all systems on our earth. That brings a growing consciousness of responsibilities upon which our very survival depends.

The properly functioning person makes his unique contribution to the operation of the entire system. He uses his inborn capacity to perceive reality. When the realities of a situation are accurately perceived, he is able to make a proper response to the demands of that situation. He also understands that there is a right direction for human progress which is discoverable and attainable. Correct perception of the relationship between what is and what ought to be frees one from illusions.

Such a person freely accepts responsibility for fulfilling his part in the whole process. His allegiance to the system, of which he is a functioning part, claims his total loyalty because he appreciates its supreme value. He sees written into its very structure the three basic values of truth, beauty and goodness. Because of the depth of his perception, he functions from a basis of concern, both for his companions in the life process, and for the well-being of the whole system upon which his own individual well-being depends. Having transcended egocentricity he responds with creative initiative to the needs of the situations he encounters.

For the best functioning of this enlightened human being, it is a great help to be associated with other enlightened people, working toward mankind's common goal. Fortunately, however, he can function alone, if that is necessary, although at a level below the ideal. Today our crisis is so great, so deep, so all-inclusive, that hope for a viable total environment for all mankind depends upon a rapid growth in numbers of enlightened human beings working together in full cooperation.

What are some of the specific aspects of the realities that the correctly functioning person perceives and acts upon? Just what does he see and respond to?

First of all, he sees that he is inescapably subject to the laws of the universe he inhabits. These are the fundamental laws of cause and effect. He has come to terms with the basic fact that he is totally subject to something other than himself, that it is impossible for him to have things his own way. If he chooses to live, there are physical requirements. He must breathe. He must eat. And he knows there are psychological laws to be obeyed as well. It is also clear to him that he cannot choose his life goal. That goal has already been written for him into the structure of the universe. His only choice is whether he will move toward it or away from it, whether he will obey or rebel. When we really perceive the structure of the system to which we belong, we see that we have *no* choice. Man must move toward the full realization of his inborn potential, toward what he was created to be. Otherwise, he ends up in frustration and meaninglessness.

Second, he sees, in all their stark reality, the current threats to mankind's survival. He perceives the effects these threats have produced, and are continuing to produce, on the physical and psychological environment within which we live. And he is aware that mankind's very survival depends upon drastic measures of correction.

Third, he recognizes his own relationship of dependency upon the entire system and his responsibility to it. Consequently he sees how he must act for the greatest good of the whole.

Fourth, and most fundamentally, he has a spiritual, mystic, sustaining relationship with a *Source* of insight and power, which in ways beyond his understanding informs, energizes and validates his life. Putting it another way, he is a religious person. Therefore, he accepts the authority of the Ultimate Reality, of God, of the supreme values of truth, beauty, and goodness.

Compare now the functioning of this enlightened, creatively initiating person with that of the ordinary egocentric person, who operates from the base of his existential self.

We have already seen that the existential self is a *structure* which operates under illusion. This false self believes that it can choose its own goals and be reasonably successful in achieving them. It believes that it can have things the way it wants them, and having achieved that, it will then be really "living". The *function* of this existential self is to maintain itself in this false and illusory identity against all threats. Acting thus under illusion, the existential self sets goals which it believes desirable. These are generally for a much shorter term than long-range lifetime goals, and are often somewhat vaguely defined, such as "happiness", a "nice family", "enough money", etc.

If a person, acting under these illusions, has clearly defined his goals, and if he is determined, disciplined, and truly dedicated to their achievement, he will probably realize them. This is the experience and testimony of great numbers of people who have achieved many things. It is a widely held and publicized faith. But it is also true, though not nearly so well understood and publicized, that, once achieved, these narrower goals of the existential self do not really satisfy the basic human drive for meaning. Dissatisfaction eventually sets in, even if for a time the achievement seems to yield significance. At this point there are several possibilities.

The individual may conclude that he has not had enough of whatever it is he has been working for. Therefore more of the same is needed, and he continues to push on further in the same direction. Or he may decide that he selected the wrong goal, so he chooses a different one and directs his energies toward that. Or it may be that by now, having followed one or both of these procedures several times, each time with the resulting dissatisfaction with his success, he has come near the end of his life span with his deepest yearnings unfulfilled. Not perceiving the essential nature of his problem, and despairing of finding any real meaning, he is likely to settle into a frustrated cynical apathy, because he concludes that there is no meaning to be had, or at least that he is not going to find it. Meanwhile he may seek to maintain an outer appearance of success which helps perpetuate the illusion among his fellow travellers on the journey.

The reality is that there is no "right" function of the egocentric existential self; its functioning is inevitably self defeating. And that is a reality for which we can be grateful. For, though painful, it is another assurance of the dependability of the underlying principles, the laws of relationship which govern the entire system.

There is another possible outcome for the traveller who starts out with the existential structure of the ordinary egocentric person. In his search for meaning he may have encountered some person, experience, book, or other expression of the governing truth, that has broken through the barriers of his egocentric shell, registered in his consciousness, given him hope and inspiration, and led him to embark upon the correct path. Such an outcome depends upon such factors as his openness to new ideas, the seriousness of his search, the timing of events, and various elements of his conditioning and experience. Most basically, however, this outcome rests upon his willingness to pay whatever price is required for the realization of the most worthwhile goal in life. This willingness is a matter of decision, of commitment, of totality of intention.

It is important to understand how the illusions of the egocentric existential self operate in the process of *character* formation. Their manifestations are all too familiar, but the processes by which these are produced are not so obvious. Their roots are grounded in ignorance. Ignorance of the true predetermined goal of man, his destiny and correct function. Ignorance of his inborn perceptive capacity. Ignorance of the fact of his conditioning, its depth, and its effect in obscuring his perception of reality and giving him a false system of values. These values are false because, as we have seen, their pursuit leads not to self fulfillment but to outcomes such as defeat, frustration, apathy, despair, or the cynicism which concludes that there is no plan or purpose in Creation and therefore no meaning to existence.

SOURCE OF GREED AND FEAR

The most fundamental illusion of the existential self is that this self must be preserved and protected at all costs. The basic drive to survive becomes a "self-protective drive", causing defensive reactions to all threats to any of the elements which make up that false self.

The self-protective drive seeks security and safety for both parts of the existential self, the physical and the psychological. Its security is regarded as resting upon an adequate supply of whatever is believed to be needed for its functioning and protection. The distorting characteristic of *greed* stems from the desire for that security. We know that everybody needs food, drink, shelter, clothing. But we view "security" as requiring a sufficient accumulation of these to last for a lifetime. Money, as the medium of exchange, can buy all these needs, so the effort is to lay up a sufficient hoard to provide that security. Since the existential self seldom feels that it has enough of anything, the pursuit of money becomes a never-ending life-long drive.

Greed is manifested in three principal forms: addictions, possessions, and pretensions. The *addictions* have to do with what have been called *"the things of the flesh"*. Here, as in all three aspects, it is important to distinguish between *needs* and *greeds*. One's needs make legitimate demands for attention. Greed for anything goes beyond need, and takes time, attention, and effort from more important concerns. May not the importance attached to food and drink by the gourmet be properly called an addiction, and classed as greed rather than need? Among "the things of the flesh", various greeds in the form of addictions demand attention and effort far beyond what is really needed by the body for efficient functioning. These lead toward all sorts of excesses of sensual desires such as the satisfaction and excitement sought through food, drink, sex and drugs. The blind alleys leading away from the path of self-fulfillment are myriad and alluring. It takes perception, wisdom and discipline to avoid being led away from our main goal by the innumerable distractions which our contemporary world offers.

We need not catalog here the vast array of things which our affluent society includes within the drive for material *possessions*. Our consciousness is constantly battered by advertising, in all the media of communication, hired by those who seek to transfer money from our pockets to theirs. To meditate at length upon the slavery to the greed for possessions, toward which our environment constantly pushes us, can be an illuminating daily exercise. It can help toward awareness of the falsity of the values pressed upon us from all sides.

Pretensions, our psychological greeds, make up the most subtle of the three forms. These drive us to seek the approval of others, prestige, status, influence over people and events, achievement, reputation, credit for good deeds, charm, charisma, etc. Because of its subtlety this is the most elusive form of greed, and the most difficult to track down and eliminate.

The threat of the loss of any of these assumed needs, or of the failure to secure them, produces *fear*. Hence the cure for fear lies in the elimination of its cause, *greed*. That can be accomplished only through the attitude of detachment discussed in Chapter III.

When one considers the troubles existing among people, one comes to perceive that the twin evils of greed and fear, stemming from ignorance, are the basic causes of the problems that bedevil us. From them come murder and all other forms of violence, war, hatred, rape and all sexual aberrations, envy, lying, cheating, corruption in government and business, stealing in all its manifold forms, social and personal responsibility, and the proliferation of more ignorance.

Questions and Exercises for Meditation

1. Introspect deeply to discover in what areas you find yourself motivated by greed.
2. Consider the extent to which a relationship between greed and fear exists in these areas.
3. What do you really fear?
4. What feelings are evoked in you by the proposal to detach yourself from the objects of your various greeds?

DIALOGUE: PROCESS OF DISCOVERY

Seek and ye shall find.
Ask and ye shall receive.
Knock and it shall be opened unto you.

Jesus of Nazareth

Discovery of truth, of reality, of what needs to be done to serve the goal, involves *dialogue*—asking questions, probing, investigating, testing. That is the essence of the scientific method which has brought us so far in discovering important relationships that exist in the physical world. Science has made fantastic gains in knowledge in the field of material nature by using that method. It is the specific venture of science to reduce mystery to knowledge. But scientists find that the more we learn, the more there is yet to be discovered. Further mystery seems always to lurk behind our discoveries. Inevitably, if we push far enough, we come up against *ultimate mystery* beyond our present human power to understand. The questions asked by science deal with the "how", what the existing relationships are, the way the cause-and-effect relationships work in any particular area under investigation. The "*why*" always leads into mystery.

The truly scientific spirit is one of openness to *truth*. It demands the willingness to pursue truth relentlessly, and to follow wherever it leads at whatever cost. The cost includes letting go our prejudices and preconceptions, and especially the precious theories and hypotheses that we believe to be fresh and wonderful insights into reality. The scientific venture demands the attitude of detachment which we have discussed. We have seen that this is attainable only by commitment to a value so high as to demand one's total loyalty. In the case of science this value is abstract *truth*. A necessary accompaniment of that attitude is its corollary, *humility*. This is the willing acceptance of the fact that we are totally subject to something greater than ourselves. It also requires acceptance of the fact that there are mysteries which presently are, and may always be, beyond our human powers of understanding.

In the seven-aspect system within which we operate, the purpose and function of dialogue is to discover what is needed in any particular situation, and how the needs are to be met. This must always be with reference to the goal of the entire process, which it is necessary to keep constantly in view. It is so easy, and so common an experience to fall into the trap which George Santayana has called fanaticism. He describes a fanatic as a person who, having lost sight of his objective, redoubles his efforts. Truly, eternal vigilance is the price of safety from the traps along our path!

The correct built-in goal for *homo sapiens* has two aspects, the individual and the social. The individual goal is fulfillment. That involves enlightenment, self-realization, psychological and spiritual maturity, love, responsibility, and creative initiative. The social goal is achievement of a total environment—physical, mental, psychological and spiritual—which is most conducive to every person's attaining the individual goal.

The necessary attitude of detachment, of objectivity, of transcendence of egocentricity is both an outcome of the process itself and also a condition for its successful operation. This seemingly circular process is partly what makes it so elusive. It seems to be both the goal itself and the *means* for reaching that goal. The principle is that of the "great paradox", already discussed. It is the principle of *giving* rather than getting, of *selflessness* rather than selfishness. The familiar statement that it is more blessed to give than to receive is true. The "blessedness" consists in the deep satisfaction of functioning fully and cooperatively, with creative initiative, in the human advance toward fulfillment.

Dialogue, then, is the process of inquiring, asking, probing to discover what is right to be done in any particular situation. Its function is to discover both *what* are the *needs* of that situation, in terms of relevancy to the goal, and *how* they can be met.

The activity of *Dialogue* falls within the domain of the feminine function. That is the open, receptive, inner function of perception and internalization of relevant truth. The masculine function is expressed in the outer thrust of appropriate action, guided, illumined, and inspired by the truth revealed through dialogue. That action falls within the category of

Method which will be discussed further in the next chapters. In these there will also be further discussion of the masculine and feminine components inherent in every human being, those faculties which need to be brought to full effectiveness in each individual if wholeness is to be realized.

PERCEPTIONS, PROCEDURES, OUTCOMES

It is natural and appropriate to ask, "Dialogue with *whom* or *what?* Whom does one *ask?* From whom does one *seek* to know? On what door does one *knock?*

It seems reasonable to answer that the first place where one looks for help is the very situation in which one is involved. What really *is* the situation? What are the problems it presents? Certainly it is true that to answer any question creatively, the first step is to be very clear just what the question is. When that is achieved, it often makes the answer obvious. At the very least it starts the seeker on his journey properly aware of his immediate goal.

Obviously, one's associates in any venture should be consulted and their perceptions shared. There is great value in open and honest group discussion among people who are committed to truth and to the solution of the common problem. The half-thought-out tentative idea of one member, if shared, can often stimulate insights or creative trains of thought in others. In free discussion by a committed group, the whole frequently proves to be greater than the sum of the parts. This is an important principle of cooperative creative activity. The small and intimate group of two in the marriage relationship can be one of the most fruitful of all, if the two partners are deeply committed to the ultimate goal and to each other. The potentialities of this relationship are the subject of further discussion in later chapters.

Finally, help is available from a source, or sources, beyond the purely human, through the media of prayer and meditation. This is a very large area of investigation. It deals with the subject called *mysticism,* which like *religion* is much misunderstood. Let us say very briefly, by way of definition, that the truly mystical experience is a *direct experience* of Reality, of God, of that which is ultimate. It involves, among other things, direct cognition, direct perception, of relevant truth. It involves rigorous discipline, a crucial fact frequently overlooked. Appendix E suggests some references for those who wish to undertake further reading in this field.

Just now we will limit our consideration to some practical suggestions for procedure. The words "*prayer*" and "*meditation*" are familiar. We have already made brief mention of one form of meditation. We referred to a process by which the feeling component of perception can be brought into harmony with truth that is already apprehended at the rational level.

Another aspect of meditation, useful here, is that of quiet waiting, with the mind open to receive an impression, an insight, a clue to the problem at hand. This has been well described as *alert passivity*. It is a state of selective receptivity. For successful resort to this process one essential condition has to be met: one's "homework" on the problem must have been done. Only then, when one has gathered the relevant data and exhausted the other available resources for a solution, does it seem promising to seek help in this way. A familiar example of the use of this process is that of Sir Isaac Newton, the falling apple, and the law of gravitation. Gerald Heard has given to this "break-through" process the name *integral thought,* as distinguished from the ordinary rational process which he called *analytical thought.* It is the process by which most of the important break-throughs seem to have occurred, whether in art, in science, or in some other area of creativity. The religious quest leads inevitably to this form of outreach, but, like any other discipline, the beginning is in small steps, not in some spectacular big leap. Any worthwhile goal demands dedicated discipline and persistence. The most important of all human goals can hardly be expected to require less.

The word *prayer* is used in a variety of ways. Some use it to cover a large area of outreach in which meditation is but one division. Others limit its use to a narrower area of petition, affirmation, or expression of gratitude, awe, wonder, or worship. We shall use it here in the limited petitionary sense of *asking, seeking, knocking,* for the purpose of discovering truth in a particular area of immediate concern. In that use it is addressed to a source of knowledge, wisdom and purpose higher than the purely human. We have already affirmed a faith in such a source. And that faith is the result of the study, the thinking, the meditation, the prayer, and the experience of many, upon which this book is based.

If one is going to use prayer, one fundamental matter must be considered. That is the attitude of the one who prays toward that to which or to whom the prayer is addressed. Is the one who prays willing to accept and act on the truth discovered—once it is seen to *be* truth? Is one willing to be obedient to the ultimate authority of Truth and Goodness? Prayer is serious business, not to be taken lightly or merely played with. Idle curiosity won't do. The promise, "Seek and ye shall find", has its governing conditions. For the scientist who searches for specific truths, complete commitment to abstract Truth in advance is the condition upon which discovery depends. In prayer, commitment to right action *in advance* is the condition precedent to discovery of what *is* the right action in the specific situation. We have already seen that there is a practical test for what is *right.* What is called for is not "blind faith". What is required is the *faith* which results in *action* on what one has come to see and believe to be true. Faith has been well described as action on one's beliefs in such a way as to govern one's life style. And wisdom requires that one's beliefs be grounded on reality, not on illusion.

Answer to prayer comes in many different ways. It is not likely to come in the form of the "voices" reported by Joan of Arc. It may come in the form of an insight resulting from a chance meeting with a stranger on the street. Or it may come in conversation with a fellow worker, or with husband, or wife, or children. Or it may be found, seemingly by sheer coincidence, in a phone call, or in a passage in a book taken idly from one's bookshelf without any intention of seeking an answer there. There are myriad ways in which the open and dedicated mind may gain access to illumination on a matter at hand.

RESISTANCE vs. RESPONSE

One further element in the process needs to be discussed. This has to do with the difference between the attitudes of response and resistance. Resistance is a fatal impediment both to the perception of truth and to right action. It is the attitude and posture of closing off, of opposing, of refusing to face and accept the reality of a situation. Acceptance of a reality does not mean that it is held to be desirable or good. It means simply that the fact of its existence is faced and acknowledged. When we do that, we are able to see it exactly for what it is. Then we are in a position to respond to the *need* of the situation by moving creatively to improve it. The feminine and masculine components of the psyche are then operating successfully in the steps of *dialogue* and *method.*

Resistance epitomizes the closed mind, the absence of the scientific spirit of honest dialogue. *Response,* the opposite of resistance, doesn't waste time saying, "It shouldn't be!", because it *is,* or, "I can't take it!" because I *have to* "take it"; it's *there!* So, in *response* we look at whatever the situation is squarely, honestly, perceptively. We take in all we can of its implications, however ugly or evil, and then take positive, corrective action. Resistance is negative; response is positive. Resistance is regressive, the way of Death; response is progressive, the way of Life.

Resistance is the reaction of the conditioned, existential self against something distasteful and threatening, something that challenges a person's attachments. It is a defensive reaction which seeks to protect what is threatened. As its opposite, response is the attitude of openness to the situation, the willingness to see it as it is, and then to make the most creative, loving response to it—the response which will move the whole situation as far as possible toward the most creative and positive outcome. Resistance leads to negative action or to non-action. Response calls forth positive action, grounded in good will. Responsibility is the ability to respond correctly ("response—ability"), in thought, feeling, and action, to the needs of a situation.

We have already seen that the egocentric existential self operates under the illusion that it must be preserved and protected at all costs. The truth is that it

must "die", if the essential self is to be freed to function fully. But the illusion, under which the existential self functions, automatically raises resistance to any and all challenges to that illusion.

Constant vigilance therefore has to be exercised to detect resistance when it arises and immediately to drop it, to open the mind to the truth. That may result in capitulation, and that is to crucify the self-will. Pride must be annihilated. All of that is painful, so the temptation is to resist. These are the negative aspects which must be dealt with in order that the positive can take over. It is like the night before the dawn, winter before spring, death before rebirth, crucifixion before resurrection. Because it all seems negative, it has been called the *via negativa.* It is really negative only in the same way that slum clearance, in order to build better housing for the people, is negative.

The positive opposites of resistance, rigidity and tightness are response, openness, giving, sharing, love. There is nothing in human experience more worthwhile and rewarding than love. Its essence is deep caring. At its highest level it involves the perception of such high value in what is loved that the lover holds himself willingly expendable for the well being of the beloved. He "loses himself" in the total, all-out giving of himself for the realization of that well-being.

When the scientist truly loves truth, he loses himself in his dedication to it. The true artist loses himself in his love of beauty, and the saint loses himself—and thereby finds himself—in his love of goodness, of God. Truth has to do with reality, with the way things are, and is basic for right action. Beauty has to do with aesthetic appreciation. Goodness is a quality of the human spirit..It is manifested in good will toward the whole system of creation, toward everyone and everything in it. It is the spirit which is unwilling to do any harm, and when it is enlightened by truth it can do no harm. The combination of *Truth and Spirit* characterizes the enlightened human being. It is what we mean by *love* in its full significance.

Action on the truth discovered through dialogue is the discipline required by that aspect of the life process which we have called "Method". That subject is developed in the next chapter.

Questions and Exercises for Meditation

1. Recall experiences of "integral thought" which you have had, instances in which answers to problems have come to you in unexpected ways.
2. What common factors do you see in those experiences?
3. Evaluate your own experience in the practice of prayer and meditation.
4. Think of situations which you met with "response", and of others to which you reacted with "resistance." How do you *feel* and what do you *think* about the way you dealt with each situation?

CHAPTER V

Landmarks Of The Way

VALUES AND REALITY

Our life outcomes depend on the choices and decisions we make, and these are determined by the values we hold. Our values are whatever we regard as important and worthwhile. All of us have our own individual value structures. These have been built up both consciously and unconsciously. Many of our values came unconsciously from our conditioning, others we have chosen consciously as a result of experience. Whatever their source, the values we hold are crucial, for they determine the decisions which set the direction for our lives.

The right value system for man is not a matter of opinion or chance; it is written into the structure of reality and can be discovered. Fortunately, for our own discovery we need not waste time or effort in exploring blind alleys. Maps and guideposts have been provided by people who have successfully travelled the route.

We have said that the entire venture with which this book deals is religious, and have explained in the Introduction and Appendix A what we meant by that statement. Therefore, we should expect to find that maps and instructions for the journey have been made by the authentic religious geniuses of our history. But how can we know who these are? Which ones can we trust?

The best we can do at the beginning is to give credence to the judgment of people who are generally accepted as trustworthy. One who is accepted as a religious genius is Jesus of Nazareth. We shall examine the map and directions he provided.

We are dealing with the subject of values because we are concerned with the answer to the dependent question: what must we do? Since what we do is determined by our value structure, that is a relevant focus for our attention. We need to discover the correct values to build into our system, so that we can make the *right* decisions for action. Those are the decisions that lead to our goal, which is self-fulfillment.

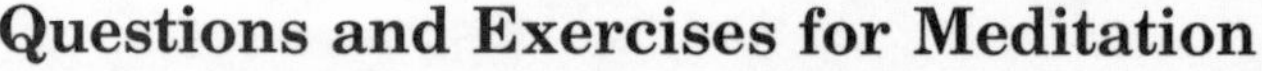

Questions and Exercises for Meditation

1. Make a list of ten values you consider important and then try to rate them in their order of importance.

2. Why do you regard these as important? Try writing out your thoughts and feelings about them.
3. Try to discover the sources which led to your including these in your value structure. Consider as possible sources: parents, teachers, peers, fellow workers, general social mores, independent judgment, personal experience.

WHAT IS FAITH?

When we come to religious matters, many of us have been told that we must "have faith", that there are things we have to "take on faith". But the modern sophisticated, scientifically oriented person has trouble with such instructions. He wants to maintain his hard-won intellectual integrity when he seeks to enter the temple of the spirit. However, there is a necessary element which we can properly call *faith*. But it is not the "blind faith" which demands that we *believe* certain propositions on which we do not find the evidence persuasive. A remark attributed to Dean Inge is interesting: "Faith is not sitting down on a chair that isn't there. Faith is the choice of the nobler hypothesis." The less noble hypothesis is that of the cynic whose view Shakespeare has captured in the words spoken by Macbeth: "Life is a tale told by an idiot, full of sound and fury, signifying nothing." The "nobler hypothesis" holds that life does have meaning, discoverable by anyone who seeks it earnestly, wholeheartedly, patiently, and persistently.

Faith is not jumping from an airplane without a parachute. When jumping *with* a parachute, the faith element enters when you are confident that it is going to open when you pull the cord, because you know it has been carefully checked and tested. Faith is based on knowledge, not ignorance. Faith is the opposite of fear. Faith looks forward to a positive outcome, fear looks forward to a negative one. Faith is a predisposition to action. It is an attitude that enables you to move, to add the increment that is not yet known. The more knowledge you have, the more faith you have.

In the seven-aspect system of the life process, discussed in Chapter IV, *method* is the act of faith, because what is discovered through dialogue is put into action. By that action new situations emerge which call for fresh dialogue and ensuing action. The process constantly leads into new experiences and discoveries. It is not a static or discontinuous process, but one which is dynamic, continuous and life-long. It results in constant improvement through disciplined action. It is an evolution in consciousness.

The ultimate values which inform and illuminate the life process are two: the individual value (and goal) of self fulfillment, and the *social* value (and goal) of the "good society". The good society is that total environment most conducive to the attainment of the individual goal by every human being on the planet.

Questions and Exercises for Meditation

1. Ponder and write out the beliefs you hold that qualify as elements of your faith. This exercise can be helpful toward your coming to know yourself.
2. Consider the evidence on which those beliefs are based. Is it reliable? Do your beliefs stand the test of logic? Do they hold up in everyday living?

THE RELIGIOUS WAY

When we seek to have "dialogue" with Jesus, it is the Jesus of history, not the Christ of Christianity we are addressing. These are not the same. To distinguish the former from the latter, we have had to resort to critical and objective studies of the available records of the life and teaching of the historical Jesus. The details of such scholarly studies are too extensive to be included in this book. Three comments, however, should be made.

One. We quote statements of Jesus in the belief that the quotations we use represent, if not his exact words, at least the *content* of his thoughts.

Two. Jesus himself was not a Christian. Christianity is a religion and a theology *about* him. He was a religious genius, a Jew, who carefully evaluated his heritage with penetrating insight. He carried the deepest perceptions of that heritage to a new level of understanding and action. Cogent evidence is available to support these statements, but its extensive study goes beyond the scope of this book. Appendix F gives some references and suggestions for investigating these conclusions.

Three. We take statements of Jesus seriously *not* merely because he made them. Their truth does not rest on the authority of Jesus. If Jesus said these things, we are confident that he said them because he saw them to be true. We can verify their truth by applying the test of experience in our own lives.

How does Jesus answer our most basic and practical question: What must we do? He was asked the question by two contemporary religious authorities, called *scribes* or lawyers, men who were learned in the Jewish law. Each of these inquired differently and in other language than we have been using, but we shall attempt to show that their questions are the same as ours. Both received the same answer. It is the answer to our basic question, provided we understand its meaning.

> And behold, a certain lawyer stood up and tempted him, saying, Teacher, what shall I do to inherit eternal life? And he said unto him, What is written in the law? How readest thou? And he answering said, Thou shalt love the Lord thy God with all thy heart, and with all thy soul, and with all thy strength, and with all thy mind; and thy neighbor as thyself. And he said unto him, Thou hast answered right: this do and thou shalt live.
>
> —Luke 10:25–28

> And one of the scribes came, and heard them questioning together, and knowing that he had answered them well, asked him, What commandment is the first of all? Jesus answered, The first is, Hear, O Israel; The Lord our God, the Lord is one: and thou shalt love the Lord thy God with all thy heart, and with all thy soul, and with all thy mind, and with all

> thy strength. The second one is this, Thou shalt love thy neighbor as thyself. There is none other commandment greater than these.
>
> And the scribe said unto him, Of a truth, Teacher thou hast well said that he is one; and there is none other but he: and to love him with all the heart, and with all the understanding, and with all the strength, and to love his neighbor as himself, is much more than all whole burnt offerings and sacrifices.
>
> And when Jesus saw that he answered discreetly, he said unto him, Thou art not far from the kingdom of God.
>
> —Mark 12: 28–34

To understand the answer of Jesus and its practical application, we need to note several things:

First. This is a two-part answer from the Torah, that part of the Jewish scriptures known as the "five books of the law", also known as the Pentateuch in the Old Testament of the Bible.

Second. In the answer attributed to both Jesus and the lawyer, there was a significant addition not in the Torah. That was the phrase, "with all thy mind". This calls for the use of the critical faculties of the mind when embarking on the religious way.

Third. In the second episode the questioner asked "What commandment is first of all?" He is asking what occupies the position of first importance in obedience to God, to the highest authority, to *Ultimate Reality*. The use of the word *commandment* is significant. The central feature of the Jewish law, the Decalogue or Ten Commandments, had to do with human conduct. Obedience to these rules of conduct was believed to be commanded by God who, tradition said, had created the world, and man, and had given man "dominion over all the earth". The Creator was represented in the tradition as being concerned with the well-being of the total creation. Through Moses, he had, therefore, given the people a body of laws, in which the Ten Commandments were central, to govern their conduct. Obedience to these would help produce a good society, which would make for man's well being.

Fourth. When the lawyer was asked to find the answer to his question in the law, he answered with penetrating wisdom. He had put his question in terms of the specific action required to "inherit eternal life". Jesus approved his response by saying, "Thou hast answered right: This do and thou shalt live". He does not use the word "eternal" in his response. Jesus is referring to a *quality* and depth of life, rather than *duration.* It is the quality of living in the "eternal now", the quality of total presence, of being integrated and free from inner conflict, of being fully functioning, of living life at its highest level.

Fifth. In view of Christian dogma, it is noteworthy that Jesus approves the answer derived by the lawyer from the Jewish scriptures. Jesus did not add the requirement of any importance placed upon himself or of holding any *belief* about him. The answer taken from the scriptures he regarded as sufficient, *if obeyed.* "This *do*!" He himself, in the second episode, gave the same answer in what are called "the two great commandments of Jesus". It is important to note that these two are not among the "Ten Commandments".

Sixth. The word *all* is used in connection with each of the four elements regarded as comprising the total person. Totality is required in loyalty to God, to the highest.

It will be helpful to take account of some other relevant statements of Jesus.

> Not every one that saith unto me, Lord, Lord, shall enter into the kingdom of God; but he that doeth the will of my Father.
>
> I say unto you, that except your righteousness shall exceed the righteousness of the scribes and Pharisees, ye shall in no wise enter into the kingdom of God.
>
> Ye shall be sons of the Most High: for he is kind toward the unthankful and evil: he maketh his sun to rise on the evil and the good, and sendeth rain on the just and the unjust.
>
> Enter ye in by the narrow gate: for wide is the gate, and broad is the way, that leadeth to destruction, and many be they that enter in thereby. For narrow is the gate, and straitened the way, that leadeth unto life, and few be they that find it.

Jesus stated the goal of man's life to be "entrance into the kingdom of God". He stated the goal in three different ways: entrance into the kingdom of God, sonship to God, and *Life*.

Since the answers to the lawyer's questions given or approved by Jesus, were taken from the Jewish scriptures, it will be worthwhile to see how Jesus formulated his own independent answer. We see above that for entrance into the kingdom of God his instruction is, "*Do the will of God*". For the second of the two commandments his formulation is what we know as the golden rule:

> "All things therefore whatsoever ye would that men should do unto you, even so do ye also unto them."

In summary, to understand the full impact of the answer of Jesus to our basic question, several points should be considered:

1. When man appeared as a living entity on this earth, he became subject to something other and greater than himself.
2. That "something" certainly includes the whole body of natural law; man cannot successfully defy the law of gravitation or any other aspect of natural law. He has no choice but to act *within* it; in other words, to *obey* it. But that something also includes what we have called Ultimate Reality, the Most High, or God, an ultimate mystery beyond our present power of understanding.
3. Total loyalty and obedience to this Reality is, therefore, man's first order of business. That is the basic religious insight.
4. Such obedience results from perception of the supreme value and love-worthiness of the object of loyalty, and the consequent response of total love for it.
5. That attitude must be expressed in action—doing the will of God, doing what is right.

6. Doing what is right calls for deep, caring concern for the well-being of all one's fellow human beings.
7. Total involvement and identification with this creative process yields meaning and fulfillment to the individual, and assures the continued evolution in mankind of consciousness and cooperation for the benefit of all.

Questions and Exercises for Meditation

1. Consider some of the ways that your will is "pitted against" doing what is right.
2. Practice for a week treating others as you would like to be treated.
3. If everyone in the world acted this way, how would you benefit?

TOTALITY AND WHOLENESS

No servant can serve two masters: for either he will hate the one, and love the other; or else he will hold to one, and despise the other. Ye cannot serve God and mammon.

Jesus of Nazareth

Dependent on which master one serves, God or mammon, are the results: integration, wholeness, unity, presence, focus; or inner conflict, division, frustration and disillusionment. These words are suggestive of the psychological and spiritual principle involved in the above statement. We cannot be both *for* and *against.* We cannot, at one and the same time, hold an attitude of good will and one of ill will. We cannot be in a state of being which is both good and bad. We either love God with all our soul, all our mind, all our heart, and all our strength, or we do not "love God".

In two parables Jesus indicated the condition for entrance into the kingdom of God. He knew that his hearers regarded the kingdom of God as the most highly desirable of all possible goals. What they did not understand was the way of its realization.

> The kingdom of God is like unto a treasure hidden in the field; which a man found, and hid; and in his joy he goeth and selleth all that he hath, and buyeth that field.
>
> Again, the kingdom of God is like unto a man that is a merchant seeking goodly pearls; and having found one pearl of great price, he went and sold all that he had, and bought it.
>
> He that hath ears, let him hear.
>
> —Jesus of Nazareth

"All that he had": what freedom and joy in that absoluteness! It is so stark, so demanding, so uncompromising that there is no conflict. To know the absolute is to know wholeness. The logic is inexorable. A divided person is not a whole person, is not an integrated personality. Divided attention is not focused attention; it is not being wholly present.

Half-heartedness is not whole-heartedness.

"Nearly" is not "all".

"Almost there" is not "there".

"Trying" is not "doing".

"Perhaps" is not "yes".

Schizophrenia is not wholeness.

Inner conflict is not mental health.

Fifty percent or ninety-nine percent is not all, and less than all is not total.

The principle is that the religious life requires a person's all.

Nothing less will do. In this wholeness is fulfillment.

The religious commitment, the decision to do always what is right, is the condition for *entering into the kingdom of God,* for seriously embarking on *the journey of the soul,* for being *on the way,* for living in the *eternal now.* It is the life-transforming decision. It is *man's ultimate commitment.* Gregory Vlastos writes of this decision:

> "Whither do you move? With it or without it? The alternatives are simple—terrifyingly simple and clear. To compromise in this matter is to decide; to

> waver is to decide; to postpone and evade decision is to decide; to hide the matter is to decide. There is no escape. You must say yes, or no. There are a thousand ways of saying no; one way of saying yes; and no way of saying anything else."
>
> —The Religious Way

The decision is crucial: the one who makes it is never again the same. But it carries no guarantee of perfection of action. Perfection is an illusion. The only "perfection" involved is the one-hundred-percent decision, made without reservation, made with all seriousness, to do in every situation what is *right*. We repeat, "what is right" is the best thing one can discover to do in each particular situation, the *best* for the entire situation and for everyone involved in it. No one has claimed that this is easy, or that the decision is reached without a struggle. Both the initial drastic decision and continued disciplined alertness are required.

The existential, egocentric self is a persistent competitor for attention. It seeks to claim loyalty, service, and effort for itself. Hopefully, however, by pondering deeply on these matters, one comes to see that to be misled by the demands of the egocentric self is truly the way to defeat, frustration and death, not the way of life. The problems that mankind has created all stem from the failure to perceive this truth.

Total commitment to the doing of God's will, to the undivided love of God, means the decision to do what is *right* all the time, not just some of the time, in *every* situation, not just when it is convenient. What is *right,* we repeat, is what works *toward,* rather than *against,* the best outcomes for all. It is what makes for continuing the evolution of consciousness, and for the well-being of the entire planet. There can be no loss or harm to anyone in such a commitment! But how can we make sure that we really see and understand that? How can we get our companions on the journey to see and understand that simple, profound, but elusive truth? Upon that achievement truly rests the "salvation", the very survival of mankind on this planet!

THE ESSENTIAL DISCIPLINES

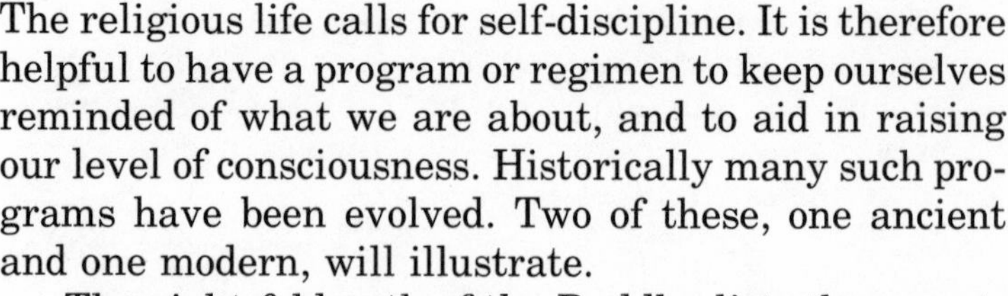

The religious life calls for self-discipline. It is therefore helpful to have a program or regimen to keep ourselves reminded of what we are about, and to aid in raising our level of consciousness. Historically many such programs have been evolved. Two of these, one ancient and one modern, will illustrate.

The eight-fold path of the Buddha lists the aspects of the life which are to be kept in line with the basic commitment: Right Understanding, Right Thought, Right Speech, Right Action, Right Livelihood, Right Effort, Right Mindfulness, Right Concentration. The value of using these as subjects for meditation should be obvious.

Right understanding, or right knowledge, means a grasp of relevant truth. This is what we have been dealing with all along in this book: the cure for the ignorance which keeps people from advancing toward the fulfillment of which they are capable.

Right thought involves intention. What do we really intend? Have we made up our minds on what we really want? That is obviously necessary before we can take intelligent action toward realizing any goal. It also involves keeping our thought processes relevant.

Right speech calls for practicing consciousness in our use of language. Are we careful to stay within the boundaries of what is true, relevant, loving, considerate? Disciplined speech, like disciplined thought, has its own practical value in what has been called "avowed intentional living".

Right action, or right behavior, hardly needs comment. Three steps in raising the level of consciousness are the three C's: conduct, character, consciousness. These begin with what has been called "the practice of the disinterested (unselfish) virtues".

Right livelihood. If the occupation in which a person makes his living is not consistent with what he professes to believe, inner conflict results. For the integral life, such inconsistency is impossible.

Right effort. This involves the will, the conscious implementation of the basic intention and decision, by the disciplined practice of openness, honesty, compassion, unselfishness, of giving rather than getting. It means keeping oneself reminded of what one is about.

Right mindfulness. The Buddha is credited with the statement, "All we are is the result of what we have thought". There is thinking which is constructive and creative, thinking which is destructive. The choice here, as in the other departments of living, is subject to one's own will. The question always is: how seriously do I desire the truly fulfilled life? Am I willing to be disciplined and aware in all departments of my life? Do I really want my essential self to be in full control?

Right concentration. This is sometimes translated "right absorption". This stresses the importance of totality, of focus, of "losing oneself" in Ultimate Reality, of holding oneself in total exposure to the light of truth and goodness. "You shall know the truth, and the truth shall make you free."

A briefly stated but extraordinarily comprehensive contemporary program for the religious life is contained in the "Twelve Steps" of Alcoholics Anonymous. Although developed to meet the specific needs of the alcoholic who wants to overcome his problem, the principles, and therefore the resulting disciplines, are universal:

1. We admitted we were powerless over alcohol—that our lives had become unmanageable.
2. Came to believe that a Power greater than ourselves could restore us to sanity.
3. Made a decision to turn our will and our lives over to the care of God as we understood Him.
4. Made a searching and fearless moral inventory of ourselves.
5. Admitted to God, to ourselves, and to another human being the exact nature of our wrongs.
6. Were entirely ready to have God remove all these defects of character.
7. Humbly asked Him to remove our shortcomings.
8. Made a list of all persons we had harmed, and became willing to make amends to them all.
9. Made direct amends to such people wherever possible, except when to do so would injure them or others.

10. Continued to take personal inventory and when we were wrong promptly admitted it.
11. Sought through prayer and meditation to improve our conscious contact with God as we understood Him, praying only for knowledge of His will for us and the power to carry that out.
12. Having had a spiritual experience as the result of these steps, we tried to carry this message to alcoholics, and to practice these principles in all our affairs.

Researchers in the study of alcoholism have pronounced the A.A. program the most successful of all the procedures dealing with that problem. But it must be added that with most people, it has been pursued only far enough to achieve stable sobriety and important rehabilitation, *not* to the level of illumination, self-realization, and the transcendence of egocentricity.

The reason is understandable. The goal of those embarking on the twelve-step program is the important survival goal of sobriety, and to recover so far as possible what has been lost. Our earlier analysis pointed out both the flaws inherent in limited short-term goals and also the basic necessity for *totality* in the commitment to *The Highest.* The twelve steps, if clearly understood, do include the essential elements, at least implicitly. The third and eleventh steps imply the first of the two great commandments of Jesus. The twelfth and several others imply the second of these two commandments. Totality is suggested, though with inadequate emphasis, by the use of the word *all* three times. But these implications can be easily missed, and, as a matter of experience, generally are. If the goal is *fulfillment*, there is no substitute for a clear understanding of the conditions to be met and total compliance with their demands.

Since this twelve-step program, properly understood, can be of invaluable assistance to one embarking upon the religious way, some further observations are relevant.

Like people generally, those with the problem of alcoholism frequently have high barriers of resistance. Like many others they are often skeptical about anything labeled "religious". In addition to having a basic authority problem, they generally have to be in desperate straits before they will ask for the help of Alcoholics Anonymous. In the formulation of the program, deep psychological insight and wise strategy led to a careful avoidance of anything which would seem like preaching or dogmatism. The twelve steps simply state what A.A. members had done to achieve the sobriety so urgently desired. The clear implication is: "We had an alcoholic problem like yours. We have conquered it and have achieved sobriety. These twelve steps are the way we did it. You can try them if you like. The decision is strictly up to you."

That is obviously intelligent strategy for those who desire to help, but realize that they will be dealing with initial resistance and skepticism. Dependency must be kept at a minimum. Understanding and wisdom, as well as compassionate concern, are necessary elements within those persons whose own experience and understanding impel them to try to share what they know with others who desperately need that knowledge.

The first of the twelve steps is based on recognition of the fact that most of those who seek the help of A.A. have suffered defeat in all efforts to solve their problem. In desperation they have had to admit defeat and seek help. That brings in the necessary element of the humility which is willing to accept help. Having asked for it and had a response from a person who has successfully solved the same kind of problem, the elements of hope and faith enter, as expressed in Step Two. The third step is the religious commitment.

The remaining steps are implementation, and include the disciplines we have been discussing. The great psychological value of unloading one's guilts through confession and restitution is recognized in Steps Four through Nine. What we have discussed in the subject of *Dialogue* is recognized in the use of prayer and meditation. The word *God,* or an equivalent, is used in six of the twelve steps. This attests to the religious nature of the process. These same twelve steps can be applied to other problems such as overindulgence in food, sex, etc.

FREEDOM AND LAW

Law is an agency of social control. In the social evolutionary process law is a necessary step out of chaos and disorder toward an ordered society. The Code of Hammurabi, the Mosaic Code, and other early codes of law, were attempts of evolving civilizations to impose standards of external conduct which would contribute to a viable social order. The purpose was to limit violence and other socially *harmful* action and, hopefully, to encourage socially *desirable* action. With its supporting institutions, the courts and the various agencies for the "administration of justice", it is intended to exercise a beneficial coercive force to regulate the conduct of people for the social good. Until human beings become wholly self-regulatory for the social good, some form of law and sanction for its enforcement will be necessary. Its ever-present limitation lies in the fact that the quality of the "justice" rendered through the law depends on the quality of the people who make and administer it.

In order to be effective in its purpose, law needs sanctions of enforcement, either those of political organization with its police powers, or those which religion is supposed to impose. At best, however, law can coerce only external conduct. One's thinking, inner attitudes, and states of being, which guide the basic functioning of a person, are beyond its practical purview. Note the content of the *Ten Commandments,* the central feature of the Mosaic Code of the Jews:

> I am the Lord thy God, which have brought thee out of the land of Egypt, out of the house of bondage.
>
> 1. Thou shalt have no other gods before me.
> 2. Thou shalt not make unto thee any graven image, or any likeness of anything that is in heaven above, or that is in the earth beneath, or that is in the water under the earth: Thou shalt not bow down thyself to them nor serve them: for I the Lord thy God am a jealous God, visiting the iniquity of the fathers upon the children unto the third and fourth generation of them that hate me; and showing mercy unto thousands of them that love me, and keep my commandments.

3. Thou shalt not take the name of the Lord thy God in vain; for the Lord will not hold him guiltless that taketh his name in vain.
4. Remember the sabbath day, to keep it holy. . .
5. Honour thy father and thy mother. . .
6. Thou shalt not kill.
7. Thou shalt not commit adultery.
8. Thou shalt not steal.
9. Thou shalt not bear false witness against thy neighbour.
10. Thou shalt not covet thy neighbour's house; thou shalt not covet thy neighbour's wife, nor his manservant, nor his maidservant, nor his ox, nor his ass, nor anything that is thy neighbour's.

—Exodus 20:2–17

The Mosaic code of the Jews was part of a legal system in which the religious and secular aspects were inseparable. There were what we could call political or human sanctions, but underlying these was the powerful religious sanction. This was seen as the functioning of an all-powerful god who demanded righteous conduct of his people, and was regarded as a source of rewards and punishments. He was believed to be subject to displeasure, anger, wrath, and vengeance, which it was highly undesirable to evoke by disobedience to his law.

The Jewish prophets were regarded as spokesmen for their god. Thus we have the term, "the law and the prophets", as representing their god's directions for righteous conduct.

When the sanctions for enforcing the law lose their power, obedience breaks down and chaos and anarchy prevail. This occurs when both "the fear of the Lord" and the administration of justice by the political authorities become inadequate to control people's actions. In this situation, *unless* people have a powerful inner authority which leads them to act for the social good without outer coercion, the results can become disastrous. The events of our time are making us acutely aware of this.

The rule of man by this *inner* authority is the essential ingredient of the "good society". Its development is the only basis of hope for man on this earth. It has been the concern of the great ones, the seers, prophets, and "saints" of history. They have provided the guide posts for our journey to fulfillment.

For the most part these have been "lonely voices crying in the wilderness". The great masses of the people have never been ready to understand and adopt their wisdom. But through the centuries, a succession of these have provided a golden thread of meaning, significance, and vision for mankind. They have been the true realists, for they have had the keen perception to understand what man has the potential to be, and what he must do to realize it.

With today's dawn of a new age, with its crisis, challenge, and opportunity, mankind is at an evolutionary nodal point in history, where people are at last beginning to look seriously for the meaning which is available.

It is important to understand what has caused the breakdown of legal sanctions. It is clear that the old religious sanction, "the fear of the Lord", is no longer effective. Sophisticated, scientifically-oriented modern man is no longer able to take seriously the primitive concept of an anthropomorphic, capricious, vengeful deity who applies the sanctions of reward and punishment.

It is also obvious that the policing of conduct by governmental authority becomes increasingly ineffective day by day. One of the obvious reasons for this is the steadily increasing magnitude of the rebellion against authority. There is a healthy psychological development, as the human being matures, in which the adolescent seeks to establish his own identity. In this effort he goes through a period of rebellion against the parental authority to which he has been subject. What we are experiencing today is more widespread, deeper, and far less healthy. Partly, this is due to extensive disillusionment with the integrity and character of so many of those in authority. A deeper cause is the broad growth of a general cynicism about any value system as having practical relationship to successful living. This is really the crux of the matter.

The three institutions upon which we have relied in the past to help individuals develop inner perception and authority, and thus establish a reality-based value structure, have become ineffective. These institutions are the home, the school and the church.

The *school,* from the pre-kindergarten level to the post-doctoral, has practically abdicated this responsibility. That is partly because the real bulwark for this educational task, the *home,* has been undergoing extensive disintegration and has consequently failed to lay the necessary foundations for the basic instructional job. The failure of the educational institutions to direct the building of sound, workable and realistic value structures is also partly due to the over-specialization of knowledge in the university. There has not been an adequate integration of that specialized knowledge into a system of wisdom having deep reality-based meaning and significance for the human venture. The *church* is largely ineffective, both because of inadequate support in the home and widespread disillusionment with religion as taught and lived today.

All of this is involved in our opening statement that the root of our dilemma is ignorance, and that the way out is through realistic, mature, and responsible education. The educational task is huge. But it can begin in any home in which people are totally commited to the religious way as that has been outlined in this book. Indeed there is no more basic or effective starting point for the educational job that must be accomplished.

STAGES OF THE JOURNEY

The contemplative orders of the Roman Catholic Church have laid out the scheme for progress in the religious life in three stages. These are called *Purgation, Proficiency,* and *Union* (with God).

Purgation is occupied with the freeing up of the essential self by detaching oneself from the conditioning which distorts and blocks perception. The experts have said that this first stage can be accomplished in three years of rigorous discipline. The egocentric self does not die easily! This book is primarily concerned with this first stage.

The second stage, *Proficiency,* as its name suggests, is that in which one is working effectively in the religious mission, with a minimum of egocentricity. It is teaching, living and demonstrating the religious way.

The third level, *Union* with God, is the highest achievement of man's life on this planet. Thus far it has been a rare achievement, attained by few persons in any historical period. But it is important to know that the experts assure us it is possible and within man's destiny.

Each of the three stages has its own level of the practice of prayer and meditation. It is at the third stage that what is called *infused contemplation* occurs. Aristotle has said that the highest activity of man is the contemplation of God. Both the levels of *proficiency* and *union* are beyond the scope of this book, but it is important for those who aspire to the very highest realization of their potential to know that these levels exist. This is the age when people need to push on to higher levels if our earth and its inhabitants are to survive. The time is *now,* to *begin* the first stage of the journey.

In purgation we do the hard work of embarking on the process and undergoing the discipline we have discussed. Illumination, enlightenment, fulfillment—the realization of our high destiny—is not usually reached in a sudden blinding flash as a gift of grace, bestowed without our preparing ourselves for it. This preparation consists of fulfilling the conditions we have attempted to set forth. Illumination may not come as a sudden, dramatic break-through. It may come quietly as a gradual, incremental gain in freedom, release, wisdom, and effectiveness. The individual's inherited temperament plays an important role in the manner in which self-realization is experienced.

SUMMARY

In the seven-aspect life process of man, *method* has been the subject of this chapter. Method is the practical action taken, once the discovery of what action is correct has been made through dialogue. Through dialogue with Jesus of Nazareth and others, we have seen the nature of that action and the governing principles, which require:

1. Total commitment to right action;
2. In each specific situation encountered, dialogue with appropriate sources of knowledge, to discover the correction action for that situation;
3. Persistent disciplined action in accordance with what is thus discovered to implement the commitment.

Persistence in this discipline leads to the establishment of right character and increasing consciousness. Expanding consciousness gives meaning to life and is itself the process of fulfillment of one's life goal.

Questions and Exercises for Meditation

1. What specific situations presently concern you?
2. What questions calling for dialogue do those situations present?
3. How do you see the disciplines outlined in this chapter applying to your situation?
4. How would a total commitment to do what is right help your situation?

CHAPTER VI

Companions On The Journey

WHAT IS LOVE?

Thou shalt love the Lord thy God with all thy heart, and with all thy soul, and with all thy strength, and with all thy mind; and thy neighbor as thyself.

Jesus of Nazareth

The single key word in both of these two great commandments is *love*. What does it mean? If we take seriously the assertion that this brief statement contains the answer to man's most basic question, we need to ponder carefully its full implication. Of the three objects we are told we must love—God, self, and neighbor—God is the most inclusive, and self the most immediate.

Let's begin with self, the most personal and insistent. What can we learn about love by considering its most immediate object? What does it mean to love oneself? We have seen that the instinctive drive for survival is built into all animals, including man. We have also seen that, in man, once survival is reasonably taken care of, his deepest desire is for meaning. In our discussion we have combined these two into a single term, *meaningful survival,* the central life goal of man. We can say that this is our highest personal value. And surely, if we love ourselves, we want whatever is the very highest personal value we can conceive of. It follows that loving oneself, then, means desiring and seeking the realization of one's destiny. And this, we have seen, is integration, wholeness, responsiveness, accurate perception, wisdom, enlightenment, fulfillment of one's highest potential. It is a matter of the utmost personal importance that we understand and continually remind ourselves that this is our inherent, built-in goal, and therefore our destiny as human beings.

We can gain further insight into the true meaning of *love* by looking at various current uses of the word. Take, first, what we mean when we talk about *falling in love*. How would we describe that experience? For the moment, remove from consideration the purely biological, physical, sexual aspects, without in any way discounting the important role these play. In much contemporary use of the word, these are given such prominence that love is often regarded as including nothing else of any significance. Actually, these are not the most important aspects of love. If we are to give the word its full significance, as being central in the achievement of meaningful survival, it must have content of far greater weight than these. Certainly, these are not involved when we speak, as we do, of loving the mountains, or the sea, or nature, or poetry, or music, or sailing, or baseball, or ice-cream! The use of the word is obviously not limited in its application to members of the opposite sex, important as that application is when we are thinking about the experience of falling in love.

Earlier we referred to the *feeling-emotional* aspect of experience. Surely this is involved when a person falls in love. Let's offer a generalized observation to consider: *Love involves an emotional or feeling response to perceived value.* In anything we say we love, we surely perceive value of some sort. The perception may be inaccurate or distorted. (We do say, "love is blind.") But whatever the perception, it is that which enables one to attach value to the object that evokes the feeling response. This, then, seems to be a basic starting point for giving real content to the word, and to the experience of loving.

A second point to observe is that we associate with love the ingredient of *acceptance*. Acceptance involves facing reality and "taking it in" without rejection or resistance. It means coming to terms with people, *as they are*. If love is to have its full meaning, total acceptance must be included. If the person still loves after seeing faults in the beloved, it is not "blind love." But if, with the new perception, the positive response is absent, it is no longer appropriate to apply the word *love* to the state of being of the erstwhile lover. It has failed to meet the test of *total acceptance.* The importance of this element must not be overlooked.

A third essential ingredient of love is a deep *concern* by the lover for the protection, preservation, and enhancement of the values seen in the love object. This concern expresses itself in a genuinely giving, even sacrificial, attitude by the lover of willingness to do whatever is necessary to ensure the well-being of that which is loved. Patriotism, love of one's nation, has led many to die for their country. In romantic literature, the lover declares to the beloved, "I would die for you!" The attitude represents a high level of self-giving, of willing self-expendability by the lover for the beloved's well-being. It is a spirit of the highest good will.

The fourth, and highest, level of love adds *courage, integrity,* and *wisdom* to the preceding ingredients. The combination of these qualities carries love beyond sentimentality into responsibility and intelligent action for the highest good of the beloved. At times such action may well cause "hurt feelings," unless the beloved has transcended egocentricity, for truth can be painful to the existential self. To love requires the courage to take risks. But the honest and loving expression of truth is often the necessary aid toward the transcendence of egocentricity and movement toward fulfillment. Only one who deeply loves is capable of the integrity, wisdom, and courage to combine truth with the spirit of good will to give the beloved the help needed toward fulfillment. Loving another as oneself, then, means not only desiring for the other what one desires for oneself. It also calls for doing all possible to help bring that desire to fulfillment.

How does all this apply to the love for God? The love for God calls for totality. It demands all one's soul, mind, heart, and strength.

We use the word *God* to designate that which is beyond description or definition. That which is ineffable, unutterable. That which is the Ultimate Reality, the Ultimate Mystery, which stands both behind and within the universe, behind Creation; that which is at once both immanent and transcendent. By the word "God" we refer to that which is source, direction, intelligence, and will; to that spirit which encompasses the supreme values of truth, beauty, and goodness; to that reality upon which we are totally dependent and to which we are totally subject; and to that before which we stand in awe, wonder, and reverence, but with which we can communicate.

God is that which draws man up toward the heights, whose plan and intention call for all of us to rise to that level of being which is our destiny and our fulfillment.

Toward that, the Most High, nothing less than totality of love, of devotion, of loyalty, can be adequate. "You become like that which you love." To love God totally is the highest activity of man. To love God totally is to "do the will of God."

Questions and Exercises for Meditation

1. Think about your experiences of
   (1) falling in love;
   (2) loving another with *acceptance;*
   (3) loving with willing *self-expendability* for the love object;
   (4) any situation of loving with spirit and truth, with integrity, wisdom, courage, and no hostility.
2. Evaluate the function and importance of love as the expression of self-fulfillment.
3. If you do not yet love God totally, consider what keeps you from doing so.

WHO IS MY ENEMY?

Ye have heard that it was said, Thou shalt love thy neighbor, and hate thine enemy: but I say unto you, Love your enemies, do good to them that hate you, bless them that curse you, pray for them that despitefully use you.

Jesus of Nazareth

The most difficult expression of "enemy" is someone who hates me, who can say nothing good about me, who, indeed, can see no good in me, and who would really like to "do me in." Jesus understood that, of all people, one's enemy is the most difficult to love. But he also understood that, for any person aspiring to self-fulfillment, it is essential to love even the enemy. He understood also, that conduct leads to character, and character is on the route to consciousness. It is therefore necessary to move with positive action toward one's enemy.

Elsewhere in his teaching, Jesus stresses the importance of the attitude of forgiveness. This is relevant here. Forgiveness is that state of inner being which understands that people are the products of their conditioning, and that they react, act, and think (in that order) from the framework of their existential state of being. From the vantage point of such understanding, one realizes that, unless people have been so fortunate as to encounter teachers or experiences leading them to clear perception, they cannot act otherwise than egocentrically. When this is understood, one does not cast blame on others for their ignorance and their resultant unenlightened action. Rather, one is able to forgive and to have an attitude of compassion, of love and concern for them. The benefit of forgiveness accrues directly, not to the person forgiven, but to the person who forgives. It is a most important level of perceptiveness on the way to self-fulfillment.

Praying for the enemy means, at the very least, holding him in a positive psychic field of good will. It involves actively projecting toward him any possible light and positive psychic power one is able to draw from the ultimate source. What this can accomplish for the enemy takes us into a field beyond the immediate scope of this book. But at least we can be assured that it can do him no harm! And it surely can do much *good* for the one who practices this discipline. It replaces what could be a negative attitude with a positive one, and thereby reduces one's own psychological stresses. If, in addition, such action turns out to be helpful to our enemy, so much the better.

Enlightenment involves love and cooperation. Praying, to the end of aiding another's progress toward enlightenment and fulfillment, is certain to aid the process for the one doing the praying. And, since prayer is the exercise of asking, seeking, knocking—of dialogue with reality—one is likely to come to the discovery of additional, positive, creative initiative one can take toward healing a negative relationship.

WHO IS MY NEIGHBOR?

A certain lawyer said unto Jesus, Who is my neighbour? Jesus made answer and said, A certain man was going down from Jerusalem to Jericho; and he fell among robbers, which both stripped him and beat him, and departed, leaving him half dead. And by chance a certain priest was going down that way: and when he saw him, he passed by on the other side. And in like manner a Levite also, when he came to the place, and saw him, passed by on the other side. But a certain Samaritan, as he journeyed, came where he was: and when he saw him, he was moved with compassion, and came to him, and bound up his wounds, pouring on them oil and wine; and he set him on his own beast, and brought him to an inn, and took care of him. And on the morrow he took out some money, and gave it to the host, and said, Take care of him; and whatsoever thou spendest more, I, when I come back again, will repay thee. Which of these three, thinkest thou, proved neighbour unto him that fell among robbers? And he said, He that shewed mercy on him.

An important and enlightening commentary on this episode comes from the Gospel of John: "For Jews have no dealings with Samaritans." This adds crucial impact to the element in the story of a hated Samaritan befriending the Jew who was in serious need. In this adroit and inoffensive way Jesus made it clear that your neighbor is anyone who has a need that you can fulfill. His race, color, nationality, creed, social or economic position, have nothing to do with his status as your neighbor. If he has a need you can fulfill, he is the neighbor you are to love as you love yourself.

In the Torah, "neighbor" clearly refers to one's fellow Jew. Jesus pushes the application far and away beyond any such limits by his strategic illustration. The criterion is the other's *need*. Love is concerned with *need*, but does not cater to another's *greed*. Wishes or desires are not necessarily needs. Anyone who truly *loves* must be intelligently discriminating between what are genuine needs and what are not. To cater to another's greeds may further obscure for him the clarity of perception he needs if he is to move toward fulfillment of his destiny.

> "All things whatsoever ye would that men should do unto you, even so do ye also unto them."

What kind of things would you want done for yourself, if you were totally committed to the highest, if you were totally committed to doing the will of God? Surely not mere trivialities, but only those things that would help you toward the goal of fulfillment. The "first commandment" is truly *first* in order of importance. It sets the basic attitude for all else. Whether it be expressed in the language of the Torah, "Love God with *All* . . . ," or in the formulation of Jesus, "Do the will of God," it provides the criterion for loving yourself, and therefore designates what you would want "that men should do unto you."

Surely by this test, violence, vengeance, retribution, and all other forms of hostility are ruled out. All negative, destructive attitudes and actions must be replaced by the spirit of good will, by a desire for the greatest fulfillment of potential for all of humanity.

Questions and Exercises for Meditation

1. Whom do you regard as enemies?
2. What can you do to remove them from that category, and change their status from enemies to neighbors?

WHO IS MY BROTHER?

"Whosoever shall do the will of God, the same is my brother and sister . . ."
". . . if thy brother sin, rebuke him . . ."

Jesus of Nazareth

In the teaching of Jesus, love is commended as the universal attitude to be taken and maintained. But the manner of its expression differs with the particular

circumstances. There are three classes of people specifically mentioned by Jesus in his teaching: the enemy, the neighbor, and the brother or sister.

For Jesus the relationship of *brotherhood* was a very precise and demanding one. To be a brother or sister of Jesus a rigorous condition had to be met. That was to be doing the will of God; it was to *be* a son or daughter of God, to be a member of the kingdom of God. All three of these expressions designate the same state of being, and Jesus used them interchangeably. Their pre-condition is the act of will, the commitment, the life-transforming decision, to do always, in every situation, what is *right*.

Among the people who have made that crucial decision, there exists the closest, deepest, most responsible relationship possible for human beings. "If thy brother sin, rebuke him." It is obviously more creative to rebuke the one you think has done something wrong than to talk with others about it. It shares with him any helpful information you have, that will enable him to make such correction as is appropriate, if your view of the situation is correct. His commitment requires that he make whatever correction is right, but it also requires that he set *you* right, if you are in error rather than he. The religious commitment requires this highest level of integrity, courage, responsibility, and caring for one another; it requires constant awareness of the basic life purpose, and keeping one's life attuned to that purpose for all mankind.

Rebuking another is generally inappropriate in relationships less responsible than that of brotherhood, or that of parent and child. It is likely to be officious and lacking in a perceptive sense of appropriateness. Consent on the part of the one being rebuked is a highly important element. But even when consent is present, the effort will be ineffectual unless there is also the commitment to *act* responsibly.

It is an important implication of all this, that one who is truly perceptive, desires fervently a great increase of the number of persons who qualify as brothers or sisters. That would mean being on the constant lookout for "neighbors" who are conscious of the need for fulfillment. One would surely want to share with them the essential life-giving truth which one has discovered and is living. That would truly be loving one's neighbor as oneself.

Questions for Meditation

1. Why is the "first commandment" first in both importance and sequence? Why is it necessary to love God totally, to hold the generalized, all-inclusive attitude of good will toward that which is ultimate, before you can love your enemy, your neighbor, and your brother?
2. If "falling in love" is a feeling-emotional experience, how can you "command" love?

MARRIAGE AND FAMILY

The relationship we have called "brotherhood" has important and far-reaching implications. It is based on the highest common *commitment*. In the language of Jesus, that commitment is to "do the will of God," which, we have seen, is to do what is *right* in every situation.

The words used in the marriage ceremony between a man and a woman come close to implying such a commitment. What if a couple entering into a marriage were truly to make the basic religious commitment to one another and to God? Surely, if made in all sincerity, that would establish firmly the most intimate of human relationships, and also the longest lasting ("until death do us part"). If such a commitment were made at the time of marriage on an increasingly wide scale, what radical transformations of our society, for the better, could be made? Traditionally, the ceremony has most commonly been enacted in a religious setting. The obvious implication is that some sort of religious attitude is involved. What if that were expressly and explicitly made central, and were taken seriously by the participants?

We have already directed attention to the breakdown of the marriage and family relationships as one of the root causes of our world crisis. The primary family is the most basic educational agency for de-

veloping fundamental understanding of the true and enduring values, upon which meaningful survival depends. Experimentation with arrangements other than the primary family for nurturing and educating the young are, as yet, inconclusive. Such experimentation in Russia, China, and Israel merits careful study. But there are strong indications that nothing is so effective in producing mature, wise, responsible human beings as the psychologically-and-spiritually-healthy primary family. That is one in which the husband-wife relationship is founded on the basic religious commitment to God and to each other. This suggests the practical social desirability of monogamous marriage of lifetime duration. This is not a currently popular doctrine. But the subject is urged as one worthy of deep and honest pondering.

Questions for Meditation

What are the individual and social implications of the following subjects?

(a) The religious commitment as a basis for resolving conflicts.
(b) The marriage commitment as a lifetime relationship.
(c) Monogamous marriage as an institution.

MASCULINE AND FEMININE

Male and female created he them.

—Genesis 1:27

If we take seriously the suggestions just made, there are further implications. What about the past, present, and future status of woman? What have we to say about women's "inferior citizenship"? What does "woman's equality" really mean? Is it right for women to be regarded as inferior to men? Is that in accordance with "the will of God"?

How does it fit into the admonition: "All things whatsoever ye would that men should do unto you, even so do ye also unto them"? What impact on this important question can be made by a fresh, open, deep and unprejudiced examination of where we have been, where we are now, and where we are going?

We have seen that there are profound stirrings of discontent among us. We are deeply dissatisfied and concerned about the threats to survival that surround us. There is a growing awareness that basic changes in our perception of reality, and in our actions, are necessary if mankind is to survive. We are emerging into a new era in which we shall either make the radical changes necessary for survival, or human history will shortly end. Among the most important elements in the whole new outlook we must achieve is that of the status of women—of *half of the human race.*

In the era from which we are now emerging, biological and functional differences between the sexes gave rise to cultural differences by which the female was assigned a status inferior to the male. We shall not make any attempt to trace the course of that development. Let us merely take note of some of its consequences. One of these has been an anomalous situation in which woman occupied, at one and the same time, a series of opposing positions.

She was both goddess, to be adored and worshipped, and whore, to be exploited for male sexual gratification.

She was both powerful and respected nurturing mother, and household slave to perform menial chores.

She was both source of inspiration and aspiration for man and the human race, and, at the same time, man's intellectual and artistic inferior.

She was the ego-and-prestige-building object of beauty for man to adorn and display to his envious fellowman, but also the dumb and inferior female.

She was the doting wife for a man to come home to, for comfort and encouragement, while he licks the wounds incurred in his daily battle with the world, but who was expected to have no human feelings, no needs to be listened to, understood or shared.

Egocentric male dominance has brought our world to the brink of disaster. This has been accomplished, we must allow, not without some female assistance, and not without apparent acquiescence by considerable numbers of women in accepting an inferior position. All along we have been referring to the dilemma of our world today, but not in terms of the primary male responsibility for it.

If the world's crisis is to be met successfully, the need is that woman shall be given, and shall take, her proper place. That place male domination has heretofore denied her. It is one of complete equality with the male of the species, in which she stands beside him in total cooperation in the human enterprise. That cooperation is one in which every person performs whatever functions are appropriate for the benefit of the whole. In achieving this equality not only must woman claim her place, but the male must make sure that it is accorded her. Together, they can make a new world.

In some circles it is fashionable to contend that all differentiation in function between men and women is culturally determined. But it seems reasonable to concede that there are particular functions which are based on sex differences. Certainly we don't see any immediate likelihood of either male child-bearing or male breast-feeding of infants. If breast-feeding is actually preferable for the well-being of the child, as some schools of thought contend, then there are at least two particular female functions which are biologically, rather than culturally, determined.

It does no damage to the claim of the rightness of total equality between men and women to concede that there may also be other functions that are more biologically than culturally determined. This would not consign either sex to an inferior role in the venture of developing truly human beings on this planet, people worthy of the designation *homo sapiens*.

There are differing human psychological capacities, some of which have come to be thought of as feminine, others as masculine. To whatever extent some of this thinking may be primarily cultural, the relationship to the corresponding biological functions seems to justify some masculine-feminine differentiation. Again, there seems to be no real danger to the cause of equality, if we continue to use the masculine-feminine labels on some of these psychological qualities. This is particularly true when we are making the point that all these qualities are inherently *available*

to both sexes, and that for psychological wholeness it is the destiny of each sex to develop both sets of qualities for full use.

In the earlier discussion of *Dialogue,* it was pointed out that this process requires employment of the *feminine* quality of openness and receptivity, the ability to be "impregnated" with perceptions of truth, or with concepts. This is the intuitive capacity of direct cognition, of direct perception of reality. And whether this quality has been developed as a result of cultural conditioning, or is an inherent feminine gift, we do recognize that it seems currently to be more prevalent among women than among men. Yet the male geniuses, who have appeared through history in many fields, have manifested this quality to a higher degree than is common. It seems not unreasonable to suggest that such people represent a higher level of human development than those who do not display this special intuitive capacity. It may also be significant that many of these whom we regard as geniuses have also displayed in high degree the "masculine" quality of initiative, of dynamic thrust. This they have used to give outward active expression to the insights gained through the "feminine" intuitional capacity. These people have displayed a better-than-ordinary integration of the two sets of qualities. Such integration is involved in the goal of wholeness, of self-fulfillment, to which all of us aspire, once we become conscious of our destiny as members of the human race.

If the marriage relationship can be based on the religious commitment to do what is right, it can be the prime setting for both sexes to learn from each other the correct functioning of the masculine and feminine qualities. Such learning can take place by observing both the correct and the aberrant functioning of these qualities, for they can be used in both ways. Detailed discussion of this subject is beyond the scope of this book but is worthy of further study. Some suggestions for this are made in Appendix G.

Questions and Exercises for Meditation

1. What personal attitudes do you have that keep equality from being realized in your life?

2. What additional responsibilities would such equality place on you?
3. What do you have to do to make your marriage and family relationships right?

STAGES OF HUMAN GROWTH

For any successful educational venture, it is important to take account of the stage of development of those being educated. At birth, the human being begins a progression through various stages of psychological evolution. The characteristic marks of these are not so obvious as those of his physical growth, but each has its important features. We seldom stop to marvel at the extraordinary progress in perception achieved by a child in the first two or three years of life. During that short span of time he is coming to terms with the strange and wonderful world into which he was thrust at birth, and with which he must learn to cope.

The detailed study of human psychological growth corresponding to the stages of physical growth is another of those interesting subjects beyond the scope of this book, important as this one is for developing wise educational procedures. For our present purpose, it will suffice to point out certain features of four principal life stages.

Stage One. In the first quarter or third of the normal life span, the movement is from the total dependency of the new-born infant to the relative independence of maturity. This time span is devoted mostly to *receiving*. This is its principal characteristic, the *taking in* of the environment in its multitudinous aspects, and the acquisition of skills needed for coping with life's challenges.

Stage Two. This second period is about as long as Stage One. It represents far less taking and receiving and more *giving*. It is during this time that mating occurs, if it has not already been accomplished, and family responsibilities are assumed. This puts the individual on the other side of the dependency scale through the need of offspring for care, nurture, and education.

Stage Three. For some twenty or more years beginning around age 45, one should be near the height of one's powers and effectiveness—giving, sharing, teaching, contributing in various ways which are expressive of concern for the whole family of mankind, and for the total environment. This moving out into larger areas of concern is greatly facilitated by the fact of being largely freed by this time from the necessity for looking after one's own children.

Stage Four. It is unfortunate that so frequently there is a deterioration in health of body and mind during the last years of a normal life span. This deterioration may not set in until some time after the customary "age of retirement", but when it occurs there can be a return to varying degrees of dependency. This can present family and society with problems of old age, ill health, senility, or other aspects of dependency. These produce feelings of general uselessness, meaninglessness, and frustration in the individual and all around him.

To deal with this "senior-citizen" problem, society has devised a variety of institutions given favorable-sounding names, such as "Leisure World". Most of these are designed to remove the individual from general circulation in "retirement homes" whose names seek to disguise the fact that they are really "old peoples' homes", where the only companionship is with others who have also moved out beyond the ability or disposition to be of further use to society. Here the inmates may play golf or bridge, or engage in other pastimes. The function of these is precisely that—to enable the participants to "pass time", without bothering others too much, until the time when they pass entirely from the scene. Or it may be that ill health has necessitated their being consigned to a "rest" or "nursing" home to spend their last days in a place where, hopefully, they will be adequately cared for until the end.

All this is a deplorable waste of human man-and-woman-power. The last years of life ought to be spent with dignity, contributing the accumulated wisdom and experience of a lifetime to the improvement of the human situation, instead of being put away, out of the mainstream of life.

One is reminded of the words of the psychiatrist, William H. Sheldon, who had made a point of the importance of preventing "the dying back of the brain" after middle age. Of those who succeeded in that venture, he said: "Fully adult minds . . . have met and made peace with reality. They have not only reclaimed the creative imagination of childhood, but have married it to understanding and have chastened it with reality. Such minds are free. In the later decades of life they grow to a power and a delight which may altogether transcend the more physically conditioned ecstasies of youth . . . having had the courage to grow up, they become the true giants of the earth."

One also recalls the example of Oliver Wendell Holmes, Jr., who served brilliantly as a justice of the United States Supreme Court into his early nineties. Or the noted professor of aeronautical engineering, William Frederick Durand, who, at the age of ninety—25 years after he had reached "official retirement" from Stanford University—was awarded a gold medal for his outstanding contribution to the jet-propulsion of airplanes. There are many striking examples of people who continued making significant contributions to the venture of living after reaching the "age of retirement". "Retirement" is a word with ominous implications.

The aged should be allowed, if they are able, to spend their last years giving back to society what they have to offer, then to depart with dignity, and have their mortal remains nourish trees or flowers—or, if they prefer, to have them returned to their original home, the sea, with no fuss made about this participation in the natural life cycle.

We have much to learn about the useful employment of human resources. Too long have we wasted untold resources of woman power. We are also wasting those of "senior-citizen power". Society can take some steps to avoid these wastes. But we have to face the fact that the creative initiative for the useful employment of those resources must finally rest on the individuals who possess them. Preparation for that employment, however, has to be made well in advance. One's life plan should take this into account at the proper time. Hopefully the preparation should begin early in *Stage Two*. Much later than that, unfortunately, seems to be generally too late!

Questions for Meditation

What do you foresee as the nature of your life activities after you reach age 50? Age 65?

THE PERSON AS SOCIAL UNIT

As water does not rise above its source, neither does a society rise above the level of the individuals who comprise it. The individual person is the social unit, the building block, of human society. *Personal* fulfillment, therefore, is the key to the building of a "good society", the "good world" of which man has always dreamed. It is only people who are mature, perceptive, responsible and loving who can guide the social changes which are essential to the existence of a "good society". It is, in other words, only genuinely religious people who can bring to realization the "good world" of man's vision.

The religious person, living in a universe of constant change, realizes that there is no such thing as a static situation. He realizes that a person who is not getting better is getting worse, because it is not possible to stand still. He therefore purposefully lines himself up with the direction of *positive* change, with that which is right, with the spirit of truth and good will. He is, in other words, committed to doing the will of God. By that commitment he enters into the Kingdom of God, becomes a son of God, willingly self-expendable. In that, he "wins his soul". He is "reborn", aligned with the vast movement of Creation toward higher and higher levels of consciousness, toward the transcendence of all egocentricity, and the release of his essential self to perceive reality accurately, and to act as it demands. It is only such a person who can be trusted to work without greed or the distortions of self-will, for the well-being of all mankind.

The important question for every human being is whether he chooses to move in that way. But he cannot make that choice unless he knows what it is. What are the conditions? What are the consequences? The person who is ignorant about this necessary choice falls unwittingly into the way that leads to frustration. And that, unfortunately, is the situation in which most people find themselves. The positive choice can only be made knowingly and intentionally. The negative choice is not really a choice at all. It is the automatic result of unconsciousness and ignorance, of not knowing that there is a positive choice which must be made if meaning and fulfillment are to be achieved.

But for this non-choice and its negative outcome there is no blame, no vengeance of an angry God, only the cause-and-effect operation of the law of a dependable universe. Ignorance does not excuse or exempt anyone from the consequences of the operation of natural law. If you step off a cliff, not knowing about the law of gravitation, your ignorance does not prevent the fall, which is the inevitable cause-and-effect consequence. Replacement of ignorance by relevant knowledge is, therefore, of the utmost importance to the human venture. It is, indeed, the crucial necessity for the continuance of man's psychological-spiritual evolution, even for our physical survival. This becomes increasingly obvious, day by day, as we become more and more aware of what we have been doing to our home, the earth.

The two crucial needs of our world are *truth* and *spirit*. Truth is the short-hand term for wisdom, knowledge, accurate perception of reality, "the way it is". Spirit is the attitude of love, of good-will, of giving. Neither is sufficient alone. Together, they define what is required of the truly human being, the person who is entitled to be called *homo sapiens*. The mature, enlightened person moves from his true perceptive center, his essential self, the ground of his being, responding to every situation he encounters consciously, perceptively, harmlessly, creatively.

Exercise for Meditation

Describe what are your hopes for your own personal fulfillment.

MISSION

Love for God and neighbor implies a concern that the will of God be done throughout all the earth. It involves a deep intention that all earth's inhabitants shall have the opportunity to be exposed to the truth, which, when acted upon, leads to fulfillment. This intention is grounded in the realization that the development of human consciousness is the highest value for mankind. It is the destiny intended for man. It is what gives meaning to his life. These insights lead inevitably to a sense of *mission*, of an inner need to spread the knowledge of the life-giving truth. When a person embarks on that mission, he has found meaning for his life. It is the answer to his basic question: "What must I do in order to attain meaning for my life, to achieve fulfillment, to realize the destiny for which I was born?"

The person who has come to true perception of reality, of the order of the universe, of God's law of truth and spirit, is impelled to share what he has discovered with all whom he can get to listen. He knows he has found the essential secret of life, and it is this knowledge that fires him with an inescapable and exciting "missionary" zeal. He moves into action, trying whatever means he can think of or discover in order to convey what he has come to know. He meets rebuffs, indifference, unwillingness to listen, even hostility—the whole range of obstacles to communication. But he knows what he knows. He has had the experience of discovering the basic truth of what life is about, and he has found meaning for his own life. So he gains experience in disciplined efforts to communicate, in dialogue, in failure and success in his efforts. Since he has found meaning for his life in his whole-hearted effort to live what he knows, there is no temptation to turn back. He understands Martin Luther's declaration, "I can do no other." The same truth is spoken to him by the poet, Robert Penn Warren: "The recognition of necessity is the beginning of freedom." He finds excitement, constantly deepening awareness, richness, beauty, significance in every moment. Increasingly he lives in "*the eternal now*." So to live is to experience the quality of "*presence*." He would not choose to be in any other time or place than where he is.

As he grows in awareness he sees more and more implications of the mission he has undertaken. He cannot with equanimity see the earth exploited and ravaged by greedy men, and thus left wasted, exhausted, despoiled and desecrated for the generations yet to come. So he works wisely and meaningfully for the well-being of the entire system, for the protection and preservation of all the earth's resources and its natural beauty. At the same time he understands that the despoilers who act out of greed are themselves the victims of ignorance. If they were not ignorant on the three basic questions we have dealt with, they would not be greedy. So the maturely religious person, while trying to prevent the damage which their greed threatens, feels for them compassion, but not hostility. Compassion does not mean consent to what is evil and harmful to the earth and its inhabitants. So he always seeks the way of positive, creative action, the way of creative intiative.

The personal and the social aspects of the religious life are inextricably intertwined and interdependent. In this chapter we have been dealing primarily with the personal aspects and with the resulting *new nature* of the religious *person.* That, we recall, is the sixth of the seven aspects of the life process which was introduced earlier. Chapter VII will deal further with the seventh aspect, *social outcome* and the application of the religious way in groups of people, ranging in size from the primary family to the entire population of Planet Earth.

Questions and Exercises for Meditation

1. Ponder whether you have a mission for your life, or desire to have one.
2. What is the nature of a mission you do, or could, desire?

CHAPTER VII

One Earth, One Humanity, One Spirit

THE HUMAN TIME LINE

Ours is the first generation to experience the awe, wonder and beauty of the planet as viewed from outer space. The reality of that vision is crystal clear. The earth is our "home" and we are floating alone in the velvet blackness of measureless space.

Viewed from the perspective of time, earth is about five billion years old. Life began in the water about two billion years ago. From that beginning, the evolutionary process has produced man, the caretaker of the planet. Compare these three time spans:

Earth	5,000,000,000 years
Life	2,000,000,000 years
Mankind's written history	6,000 years

Our written history is short, only one hundred lifetimes of sixty years each. But it is of great importance, for from it we can trace the course of our psychological and spiritual evolution, and learn what we must do now to continue the process.

Among the written records of the last six thousand years the Bible has a special relevance to any search for the way to fulfillment because of its display of the stages in mankind's psychological evolution. That relevance is universal and applicable to all mankind. It is not dependent on any person's ethnic, cultural or religious background.

The part of the world in which western mankind lives has been called Christendom, in traditional recognition of its Judeo-Christian background. That heritage necessarily has special significance for those who have been subject to its conditioning. But it also has significance for *all* the people of the planet if its clues to an understanding of the universal controlling principles can be recognized and pursued until they are mastered. Critical and radical study of that heritage enables one to perceive the direction of man's past psychological evolution, and to comprehend the principles which govern its continuance.

An understanding of the role of these principles in the biblical tradition can enlarge one's base of perception. The Bible contains both Jewish and Christian scriptures. The Jewish part, the Old Testament, covers two thousand years of history from the time of Abraham to that of Jesus. The writing was done by many people over that span of time. This Old Testament period is the first of the three historical ages with which we are concerned. We shall designate it as the *First Dispensation*.

The *Second Dispensation* is the two-thousand-year time span from Jesus to now. It is the New Testament or Christian age. All the New Testament writings were completed in the first three centuries, but their dominant influence continued throughout this second age.

The second dispensation has now come to an end and we have entered the third. The implications of each of these three ages will be dealt with in sequence.

THE FIRST DISPENSATION

In this first dispensation, man's psychological evolution and his relationships were controlled by an *external authority*. Law, in the form of the ten commandments, governed. Obedience to the law was demanded, but no inner transformation was required. The evolutionary plan for association and cohesiveness was the *clan* or *nation*.

Moses set the pattern for the Jewish people. He led them out of slavery in Egypt and formed them into a clan or nation with a special sense of obligation to obey the law. This law was believed to have been given directly to Moses by God on Mount Sinai. God is also reported to have given this clan a special mission and destiny by saying to Moses: "Thou shalt say to the house of Jacob, and tell the children of Israel: Ye have seen what I did unto the Egyptians, and how I bare you on eagle's wings, and brought you unto myself. Now, therefore, if ye will obey my voice indeed, and keep my covenant, then ye shall be a peculiar treasure unto me above all people: for all the earth is mine: *And ye shall be unto me a kingdom of priests, and a holy nation.* These are the words which thou shalt speak unto the children of Israel."

The people whose story is primarily involved in the Old Testament, the people of the first dispensation, stabilized on two aspects of the evolutionary stage of that dispensation, *law* and the *clan*. Both of these were

essentials in a passing stage of the evolutionary process, a stage of *reality,* a stage in the plan of God. But stabilization at any stage of a moving process means ultimate extinction. It can occur in various dimensions. It can take place through permanent adjustment to some specific portion of the environment, as with the creatures of the sea. It can be manifested in settling on the socio-political grouping of people in a clan or nation, or it may be fixation on the *ideology* of some phase of the evolutionary plan of God. In this case it occurred in two aspects: *the law* and the *ideology* of the separatism and exclusiveness of a "sacred clan" favored of God.

Earlier we alluded to the mystery of time. One thing we observe is that it calls for continuous change. Time and change are inseparable. We can then say that *time is change.* When we speak of something as "timeless", we mean that it is unchanging. *Life* is intimately related to time and its character also is change. The evolutionary imperative is for *inner mobility,* the capacity and willingness to respond to the evolutionary demand for change. *Stabilization is death.*

Today there are people still living in the Old Testament age who have failed to understand this principle of mobility. They stabilized on the old law, the old clan, and the old tradition. The call to a new stage is well stated by Teilhard de Chardin: "The age of nations is past. The task before us now, if we would not perish, is to build the earth."

THE SECOND DISPENSATION

The inner mobility required in the second age means that one must move to a base of authority founded on an inner transformation, a base entirely different from the rigidity of an external legal code. It also means that one must move beyond the limitations of the clan as the socio-economic basis of association. The three ages are a sequence in the evolutionary process. The second age marks the emergence of the whole individual, the person who has total inner mobility, who can be all-inclusive on the universal base of spirit and truth. Jesus was the fulfillment of this evolutionary demand to move. He was the transition figure and demonstrated the total change that each person must undergo in order to move to the universal consciousness.

The *universal cohesiveness of mankind* can occur only by humanity fulfilling its highest potential, which is to perceive reality and cooperate for the well being of the total system. This requires total transformation, and that means detachment from specific ideologies, from specific theologies, and from all man-made models and structures of reality.

Jesus taught *the way of reality*. That means to understand that there is no external authority which intervenes in human history to cause events to happen on the planet. It means that man must move to the position of realizing that *he is cause*. He causes good, and he causes evil.

It means that he must take on the life of universal religion, based on spirit and truth. It is only such a religion that all men of all races and cultures can accept. This is the only way by which our planet can be directed away from the destruction that threatens. Jesus knew that men would perceive this only if they had "ears to hear and eyes to see" that only a religion based purely on spirit and truth is universal.

The *spirit* is that of total inclusiveness, of nonviolence, of good will for all, of love, of commitment to the highest. *Truth* and *reality* are one. Truth requires the total absence of illusion, prejudice, misconception and misperception. Creative initiative can be taken in any situation only on the solid base of truth and spirit. That is the way taught and demonstrated by Jesus. It is the way to personal and social fulfillment.

At the time of Jesus, people were not ready to undergo this total transformation. Jesus was too far ahead of the people of his day for them to understand him. The world had a further time-span of experience, maturing and preparation to undergo before it would be ready.

The two thousand years of this transitional second dispensation were occupied with many things. There were the initiation, development and spread of both Christianity and Islam. The older religions such as those of China, India, and Persia were, of course, developed during the period of the first dispensation. Conquest, and the building and decay of empires, continued. The world was explored and frontiers were pushed out until there were no more on earth, and exploration of outer space began. Science claimed increasing attention in its thrust to reduce mystery to knowledge, first in the realm of material reality and later in the added inner realm of the psyche. Scientific discoveries led to a vast technological development, and with it powerful economic enterprises exploiting the technology to satisfy greed on a constantly expanding scale. The great expansion of science contributed to the reduction of superstition and faith in magic. It also brought considerable doubt and skepticism about many of the expressions of religion, as well as about religion generally and the values associated with it.

There is today a dawning realization that the movement and direction of the last two thousand years have brought our world to the brink of disaster and extinction. However, the crisis we have reached has also prepared us for the new age, the third dispensation, over whose threshold we have now stepped.

There is a new readiness to listen to truths which challenge preconceived opinions. As recently as three hundred years ago not only would this book have been burned, but its sponsors would have been put to death for heresy. Movement has taken place. Recently there has been a noticeable increase in the active search to find deeper meaning for life, and with it a growing readiness to move in the direction dictated by reality. Perception of the absolute necessity to change as a condition for survival results in impetus for the change. Increasing willingness to take constructive action gives hope that mankind is ready to make the necessary responses to the challenge of the third dispensation.

THE THIRD DISPENSATION

At various points in the long evolutionary story of man, something in the planet's timing dictated major shifts. In man's line of advance, the challenge was met every time by the proper response, the response that permitted survival and the continuation of the process of developing consciousness. Something enabled our ancient ancestors to make these correct responses before human consciousness emerged. But with the development of consciousness our evolution, no longer primarily physical, became psychological and spiritual. Its continuation depends on our conscious decision to do what is required.

Man does not choose the timing of a crisis that calls for change. It is crucial for us to understand the imperative character of the change called for, and to move with it. The crisis that confronts us at the beginning of the third dispensation is the threat of total destruction, the most critical threat that we have ever faced. But it is not inevitable that man shall now destroy the planet. That destruction will come about only if we fail to act in time with the right response.

The second dispensation called for mankind to move radically toward individual wholeness and fulfillment. It laid down and demonstrated the conditions for achieving that.

The third dispensation now demands the movement of fulfilled individuals in large numbers into the cooperative community of mankind. This is the social and global fulfillment in which the unity and beauty of cooperation, of love for one another and for all are realized. All benefit from the uniqueness of individuals and the diversity of talents, all moving to build one earth and one humanity in one spirit. The attitude of love is to be useful to others, not to amass large materialistic gains for oneself. It is to hold and use all the benefits of technology wisely for the well-being of the community of mankind.

The second dispensation was the time which called for personal fulfillment. The third dispensation is the time for community.

Since the call for personal fulfillment was not met by large numbers of people in the second dispensation, the demands of both dispensations must now be fulfilled in the third. This can be achieved as the nature of the crisis and its demands are sensed, intuited, comprehended, and the next step taken by increasing numbers of people. The crucial need is the understanding which leads to the necessary all-encompassing change.

The two aspects of the task are the personal and the global. This book has dealt primarily with the personal aspect. This obviously has to be dealt with and the individual process embarked upon before the global process of building the cooperative community of mankind can be undertaken. Human society is made up of people, and a society cannot rise any higher than its most highly developed members.

The first step in building that community is to develop a creative minority of deeply committed people, the universal human beings who have embarked on the universal religious life of spirit and truth, who have accepted the reality that this is *one earth,* that we are *one humanity,* and that we must be of *one spirit.* Such people will have assumed the personal responsibility for what is right for life in terms of the six basics: life, death, good, evil, masculine and feminine. They will understand that the basic questions to be answered by every individual are: Will he move toward wholeness, toward total individual and global fulfillment? Does he see the necessity for his participation in the goal of the third age? Does he see that fulfillment of the individual is in contributing himself to the whole?

This creative minority will have mastered the consciousness of the authority which resides in objective reality. They will have come to understand themselves to be the executors of God's plan. They will understand the abstract concepts of *being* and *goodness,* and will know that to be *good* is to understand the function of *love* as an absolute in the life. They will understand that love expresses the most all-inclusive, the most universal, the highest of all principles. But they will also understand that "universal" and "inclusive" are abstractions until fulfilled in the individual life. Finally, for the well-being of the world, they will understand the necessity for the existence of a growing community of people who have mastered and are living the universals around which mankind can unite.

The second aspect of the task is in the evolutionary development of that cooperative community. It is only that which can build the good society, the kingdom of God on earth. This must be a process of *social-*

psychological evolution. Several elements are necessarily involved.

1. People will come together in groups of varying size to work cooperatively for personal and global fulfillment through the essential educational process which we have seen to be indispensable.

2. Within each group cohesiveness, trust and cooperation will grow because of the common commitment to the universal religious life which establishes the "brotherhood" in the special sense developed in Chapter VI.

3. Individual and group discipline in conscious responsibility for the proper use of all resources will result in a wiser and better life style. The group will thus become a small-scale demonstration of the good society in attitude, action and outcome.

4. Each group needs to discover its own optimal size. When the optimal size is reached, more and more of the group's resources can be devoted to helping other groups get started.

5. Cooperation among groups in the common educational mission will build constantly increasing effectiveness in sharing, with more and more people, knowledge of the way to individual and global fulfillment, and in demonstrating it in action.

6. The ideal ultimate goal is a world in which every person is totally committed to the universal religious life of spirit and truth.

The immediate practical goal is a more modest one. The future of every one of us and of our earth rests on the attitude and actions of a creative minority of people who are living the universal religious life of spirit and truth. The assembling, motivating and education of people to become such a creative minority of informed and effective people can produce a great source of power for the good. That is the first mission to be accomplished. It requires numbers, but not such large numbers as might be supposed. The really important achievements in the civilizing process of mankind have been accomplished by small numbers of enlightened people. But the expansion of numbers by dedicated groups of people working in cooperation can be exponential.

If each of one hundred people on the path of fulfillment were to undertake to enlist five other people every year for the mission, and each person so enlisted were to do the same, in six years this would produce over a million and a half trained, dedicated and effective people with a positive power for good such as the world has never known.

If the yearly increment per worker were ten instead of five, there would be a million people in four years! If the number were only one per year for each worker, the progress would be greatly slowed down, but even then the total number in thirty-three years would be over eight billion, twice the present world population!

The educational task is arduous but it can be done. It can produce nothing but good, because of the double requirement of spirit and truth which can do no one any harm. The world's dire need demands that this mission be carried forward. The necessary knowledge is available. The need is to find the people who are ready, willing and able to be educated in the way to fulfillment.

The message to be conveyed is one of hope, excitement, inspiration, joy and fulfillment. What more could any worker ask? It calls for hard work, but the most meaningful work anyone can be engaged in. Such work is no burden. It is rather the most satisfying and meaningful of all possible activities.

SYMBOLS OF SIGNIFICANCE

Symbols are devices for representing and conveying truth and meaning to the consciousness. Words are familiar symbols which represent things, experiences, concepts and ideas. There are also wordless ways of expressing profundities by symbols, such as those appearing throughout this book.

How does a human being communicate to another an experience which has inner significance? There are

mundane experiences which have to do with the physical dimension of survival: eating and drinking, shelter from heat and cold. But there are experiences which have nothing to do with that dimension, but are experiences of *meaning*. Historically, events of profound significance for humans have often been communicated by wordless symbols.

One of the symbols of the first dispensation is the "Star of David". It symbolizes man's search for God and God's command to man that he move to realize ethical standards and adherence to the law of good character and conduct.

The six-pointed star of David is a basic Jewish symbol, and the books of the first dispensation, the Old Testament, are Jewish scriptures. The six points of this star remind us of the six universals dealt with in the first dispensation: life, death, good, evil, masculine and feminine. In this star, they are in perfect balance. The star is made up of two equilateral triangles. One of these has its apex pointed upward; this triangle symbolizes man's upreach from the earth plane, seeking to penetrate the plane of heaven, the "gnostic" plane, the plane of higher knowledge and wisdom to which man aspires. The other triangle symbolizes the heaven plane penetrating the earth plane, God seeking to find response from man to receive knowledge of the way to fulfillment.

A symbol of the second dispensation is the five-pointed star which is the conventional symbol for the stars of the heavens. It is also the star of Bethlehem which is the symbol for Jesus. It guides to the place of origins, which the manger represents, the beginning of new hope and new possibilities. The manger and the animals associated with it represent the basic nature of creatures living in obedience to the law of their being. The symbol of Madonna and child has always been positive because it represents the receptive feminine principle and the new possibility in the new-born child. The star guides the three kings, and their gifts can represent all worldly advance brought into the service of what is good.

In representing Jesus, four of the five points of the star symbolize the aspects of human personality—soul, mind, heart and strength—totally devoted to

God; the single point at the top pointing heaven-ward, symbolizes the one-pointed singleness and totality of the commitment of Jesus.

This star, then, is a symbol of completion, of wholeness. It provides the frame for Leonardo da Vinci's representation of man. It is firmly grounded on two points at the bottom, it has two points outstretched as arms, and one point at the top for the head, pointing upward and reaching for the highest, the ultimate of goodness and reality.

It is to be noted that this star, when turned upside down, has been used to represent the devil, as the face of a goat with two horns and a beard. There is significant symbolism in that fact. Man must keep his feet on the ground and his head up! The choice is between God and the "devil." There is nothing in between.

The symbol of the third age is the star of twelve rays, the twelve-spoke wheel, the "cross of fulfillment" which appears on the cover of this book. The third dispensation is the age of fulfillment. In this age the individual must attain enlightenment. He must move on from basic problems of conduct and character to the development of consciousness. This consciousness is a realization of the unity of *all* things. It understands the one fundamental law of inter-relatedness and abides by it. It responds, in recognition of the wonder of creation, to love God and one's fellow man, and to accept responsible dominion of the earth for life and the entire planet.

Each of the twelve rays of the cross of fulfillment has its meaning, and together they represent the entire spiritual journey of the individual to fulfillment. The cross is symbolic of the *community* of individuals who have chosen the spiritual way. It embraces the Old and New Testaments and the affirmation of the Great Commandments of Jesus.

The number twelve is involved in all three ages. In the first, there were the twelve tribes of Israel. In the second, Jesus had twelve disciples. Twelve also symbolizes *community,* and the third dispensation is the age of community.

The symbol on the cover of the book also has the full-circle rainbow, a highly significant symbol. The upper half is the ancient symbol representing God's covenant with Noah, promising that God would never again cause a flood to destroy mankind. Adding the lower half to complete the circle symbolizes man's return covenant that man will not destroy the earth but will take responsible dominion as caretaker in cooperation with God.

WHAT MUST I DO?

This book began with three questions, the most basic questions a person asks if he consciously intends to have his life add up to meaning—meaning to himself and meaning to those closest to him. The third of these questions, the one most immediately practical, asked what we must do to realize that meaning. This book offers an answer and ends by repeating the question—to *you!*

Questions and Exercises for Meditation

1. What must you do if your life is to have meaning?
2. What do you feel about the world you live in: Discouragement? Despair? Hope? Faith in the evolutionary process? Faith in yourself? Faith in people and their potential?
3. What do you see as your particular contribution to the world's need?

FURTHER STEPS

Creative Initiative Foundation is a non-profit educational foundation. Its purpose is to help people understand the most basic issues of life and how to deal with them creatively. The foundation is the outgrowth of more than forty years of work in this field, based on the inheritance of the sages, seers and saints of the first two dispensations. The foundation offers courses and seminars designed to forward the process which leads to fulfillment. At the present time there are several thousand people, in various parts of the United States, actively involved in teaching and living the principles set forth in this book. Information on available courses and seminars may be obtained by writing to the address below. If you are interested we should like to hear from you.

When you write, it would be helpful to us to know how this book came to your attention, and the nature of your response to it. Since our interest and activities are with *people,* we should be grateful if you would tell us something about *yourself* and your primary interests.

Creative Initiative Foundation
222 High Street
Palo Alto, California 94301

APPENDIX A:

Supplement to the Introduction

Here is some supplementary material on the nature and function of religion, in the form of suggestive statements by a number of people with widely varying intellectual backgrounds.

The psychiatrist, William H. Sheldon, remarked that:

> ". . . religious consciousness remains as native to human life as sexual consciousness or hunger consciousness. Emotional awareness of relationships in the universe which lie beyond the clear knowledge of the present point in time, constitutes religious consciousness. From the point of view of sustained happiness this is by far the most vital and significant area of awareness . . ."
>
> *Psychology And The Promethean Will*

The British physicist, Lancelot Law Whyte, declared:

> "At its root religion is an expression of man's search for unity; so also is science."
>
> *The Next Development In Man*

A university professor of literature, Herbert J. Muller, made this statement:

> "Religion might . . . be defined, broadly, as an effort to make sense of a mysterious world, and to get into satisfactory relations with the mysterious powers that control it."
>
> *The Uses of The Past*

A biblical scholar, Leroy Waterman, while Chairman of the Department of Oriental Languages and Literatures at the University of Michigan, wrote:

> "What self-preservation is to the animal, religion is to the essence of personality. Religion may thus be summarized as man's persistent endeavor to adjust the reality within him to the most significant realities without, for the purpose of preserving and enhancing the values of personality."
>
> *Religion Faces The World Crisis*

George Russell Harrison, while dean of science at the Massachusetts Institute of Technology, stated:

"The basic tenets of all great religions, the distilled spiritual wisdom of humanity (as distinguished from minor theological details, regarding which many thousands of existing creeds differ), represent closely what science is revealing. The universe is based on ordered progress, not on chaotic change. Man can improve his environment, his own nature, and his opportunities. Through cooperation new entities can be formed from lesser entities which give greater purpose and achievement to existence. There is direction to living, which gives stability in the midst of change. These things the ancient sages knew; science helps to make them apparent to us all."

What Man May Be

The philosopher-historian, Gerald Heard, wrote:

"... We might say that religion is a process of a constantly extending balance. It is that maintenance of identity with an ever-expanding change, which is the outstanding and mysterious characteristic of life itself.

"The Perennial Philosophy is, then, in essence eternal—it is the unchanging Law of man's nature. Its expression, however, changes, as man's power of expressing himself and defining his circumstances both grow in precision."

The Eternal Gospel

Walter Lippman, noted news commentator, said:

"I venture, at least, to suggest that the function of high religion is to reveal to men the quality of mature experience, that high religion is a prophesy and an anticipation of what life is like when desire is in perfect harmony with reality. It announces the discovery that men can enter into the realm of the spirit when they have outgrown all childishness."

• • •

"... the evidence converges upon the theory that what the sages have prophesied as high religion, what psychologists delineate as mature personality, and the disinterestedness which the Great Society requires for its practical fulfillment, are all of a piece, and are the basic elements of a modern morality."

A Preface to Morals

Harvard Professor of Philosophy, William Ernest Hocking, made the observation:

"... For it is only religion which, finding the ultimate solitude of the soul for which all your sociabilities and amiable grimaces are husks, can create the unpurchasable man. And it is only the man unpurchasable by any society that can create a sound society. This is the paradox which leads even the political realist to set up bills of rights which the state must not trespass upon. And the society of unpurchasable men, with a moral anchor outside their own national life, is the only society that can beget world unity."

The Atom As Moral Dictator

Psychiatrist, William L. Pelz, M.D. stated:

"Over and over again the aims of religion and psychiatry are found to be the same. To lose oneself in order to find oneself, to be mature, to put away childish things; to have good object relationships, to love one's neighbor; to live in accordance with the reality principle instead of the pleasure principle; to follow the precepts of the Sermon on the Mount—these are different ways of saying much the same sorts of things."

Adolescence In The Age of Longing

Gerald Heard made another relevant observation:

"The ethic which does not depend on a Cosmology is untrue; the Cosmology which does not result in an Ethic, a life of deduced action, is meaningless. Today our ethic has depended on an anthropomorphic cosmology and so has failed because people can no longer believe that picture of Reality to be true; while our cosmology, which has been completely mechanistic, has resulted and must result in behavior which is utterly unethical, unrighteous."

Training For The Life of The Spirit

Rufus Jones, Quaker professor of philosophy, said:

"Religion, which is man's noblest attitude and response to what is highest and purest in the universe, cannot be preserved and maintained in some watertight compartment of the mind, unaffected by the total outlook on the facts and processes and interpretations of the world as a whole. If, therefore, religion in these times is to be *vital*—and if it is not vital it is negligible—it must maintain its reality, not apart from the intellectual currents of the times, but as something unmistakably real and in complete conformity with all that we know to be *true*."

A Call To What Is Vital

Aldous Huxley wrote:

"Religion is, among other things, a system of education, by means of which human beings may train themselves, first, to make desirable changes in their own personalities and, at one remove, in society and, in the second place, to heighten consciousness and so establish more adequate relations between themselves and the universe of which they are parts."

Ends And Means

William James, who has been called the father of American psychology, in his classic study for the famous Gifford Lectures, made many thoughtful observations. Here are two:

". . . the best fruits of religious experience are the best things that history has to show. They have always been esteemed so; here if anywhere is the genuinely strenuous life; and to call to mind a succession of such examples as I have lately had to wander through, though it has been only in the reading of them, is to feel encouraged and uplifted and washed in better moral air."

• • •

"Summing up in the broadest possible way the characteristics of the religious life, as we have found them, it includes the following beliefs:

1. That the visible world is part of a more spiritual universe from which it draws its chief significance;

> 2. That union or harmonious relation with that higher universe is our true end;
>
> 3. That prayer or inner communion with the spirit thereof—be that spirit "God" or "law"—is a process wherein work is really done, and spiritual energy flows in and produces effects, psychological or material, within the phenomenal world.
>
> Religion includes also the following psychological characteristics:—
>
> 4. A new zest which adds itself like a gift to life, and takes the form either of lyrical enchantment or of appeal to earnestness and heroism.
>
> 5. An assurance of safety and a temper of peace, and, in relation to others, a preponderance of loving affections."
>
> *The Varieties of Religious Experience*

On the problem of keeping religion contemporary, the classical scholar, Edith Hamilton, has a trenchant observation:

> "One form of religion perpetually gives way to another; if religion did not change it would be dead. In the long history of man's search for God and a basis for right living, the changes almost always come as something better. Each time the new ideas appear they are seen at first as a deadly foe threatening to make religion perish from the earth; but in the end there is a deeper insight and a better life with ancient follies and prejudices gone. Then other follies and prejudices come in, and the whole process has to be gone over again."
>
> *The Greek Way To Western Civilization*

An excellent and unique anthology of readings on the religious way, and its implications, now available in a revised paperback edition, is *The Choice Is Always Ours,* edited by Dorothy Berkley Phillips, with co-editors Elizabeth Boyden Howes and Lucille M. Nixon. (Re-Quest Books, 1975).

APPENDIX B:

Supplement to Chapter I

The problem of achieving scientific certainty in psychological research has been perceptively discussed by Abraham H. Maslow:

"... So many people insist on being *either* pro-Freudian *or* anti-Freudian, pro-scientific psychology *or* anti-scientific psychology, etc. In my opinion all such loyalty-positions are silly. Our job is to integrate these various truths into the *whole* truth, which should be our only loyalty.

"It is quite clear to me that scientific methods (broadly conceived) are our only ultimate ways of being sure that we *do* have truth. But here also it is too easy to misunderstand and to fall into a pro-science or anti-science dichotomy. . .

"Science, as it is customarily conceived by the orthodox, is quite inadequate to these tasks. But I am certain that it need not limit itself to these orthodox ways. It need not abdicate from the problems of love, creativeness, value, beauty, imagination, ethics and joy, leaving these altogether to "non-scientists," to poets, prophets, priests, dramatists, artists, or diplomats. All of these people may have wonderful insights, ask the questions that need to be asked, put forth challenging hypotheses, and may even be true much of the time. But however sure *they* may be, they can never make mankind sure. They can convince only those who already agree with them, and a few more. Science is the only way we have of shoving truth down the reluctant throat. Only science can overcome characterological differences in seeing and believing. Only science can progress.

"The fact remains however that it *has* come into a kind of dead end, and (in some of its forms) *can* be seen as a threat and a danger to mankind, or at least to the highest and noblest qualities and aspirations of mankind. Many sensitive people, especially artists, are afraid that science besmirches and depresses, that it tears things apart rather than integrating them, thereby killing rather than creating.

"None of this I feel is necessary. All that is needed for science to be a help in positive human fulfillment is an enlarging and deepening of the conception of its nature, its goals and its methods."

Toward A Psychology of Being

A paper by Else Frenkel-Brunswik, from a symposium on Psychoanalysis and Scientific Method, includes this significant statement:

> "All that is considered an essential ingredient of maturity in psychoanalysis, such as rationality, the overcoming of aggression, cooperativeness, the ability to love and to work, and the courage to face inside and outside threats that oppose these characteristics, bespeak standards that stand up well among the traditional systems of ethics. In psychoanalysis every neurosis is in and by itself considered as failure at moral control."
>
> *Meaning of Psychoanalytic Concepts And Confirmation of Psychoanalytic Theories*

Erich Fromm has said:

> "My experience as a practicing psychoanalyst has confirmed my conviction that problems of ethics can not be omitted from the study of personality, either theoretically or therapeutically. The value judgments we make determine our actions, and upon their validity rests our mental health and happiness."
>
> • • •
>
> "Psychology can not be divorced from philosophy and ethics nor from sociology and economics."
>
> • • •
>
> ". . . human personality can not be understood unless we look at man in his totality, which includes his need to find an answer to the question of the meaning of his existence and to discover norms according to which he ought to live."
>
> *Man For Himself*

In his book, *Reality Therapy: A New Approach To Psychiatry,* William Glasser, M.D., sets forth a system of therapy which he has developed and found successful with a wide variety of patients having psychological disorders. It is founded on the conviction that the basis for these disorders is irresponsibility in the way the patients have sought to meet their genuine needs. The therapeutic process is designed to help the patient become responsible in his actions. When he acts responsibly the disorder is cured. Several excerpts from the book will convey the essence of the principles on which Dr. Glasser operates.

> "We believe that, regardless of how he expresses his problem, everyone who needs psychiatric treatment suffers from one basic inadequacy: he is unable to fulfill his essential needs . . . whatever the symptom, it disappears when the person's needs are successfully fulfilled."
>
> • • •
>
> "In their unsuccessful effort to fulfill their needs, no matter what behavior they choose, all patients have a common characteristic: *they all deny the reality of the world around them.*"
>
> • • •
>
> "Psychiatry must be concerned with two basic psychological needs: *the need to love and be loved and the need to feel that we are worthwhile to ourselves and to others.*"
>
> • • •
>
> "But, whether we are loved or not, *to be worthwhile we must maintain a satisfactory standard of behavior.* To do so we must learn to correct ourselves when we do wrong and to credit ourselves when we do right. If we do not evaluate our own behavior, or having evaluated it, we do not act to improve our conduct where it is below our standards, we will not fulfill our need to be worthwhile and we will suffer as acutely as when we fail to love or be loved. Morals, standards, values, or right and wrong behavior are all intimately related to the fulfillment of our need for self-worth. . ."
>
> *Reality Therapy: A New Approach To Psychiatry*

Dr. O. Hobart Mowrer, Research Professor of Psychology, University of Illinois, wrote a Foreword to Glasser's book. His own experience and research led him to similar conclusions. Two of his books are worthy of study by those who wish to go more deeply into this subject. They are *The New Group Therapy* and *The Crisis In Psychiatry And Religion*.

Two additional statements by Abraham Maslow should be included here:

> "The neurotic is not only emotionally sick—he is cognitively wrong! If health and neurosis are, respec-

tively, correct and incorrect perceptions of reality, propositions of fact and propositions of value merge in this area, and in principle, value propositions should then be empirically demonstrable rather than merely matters of taste or exhortation. For those who have wrestled with this problem it will be clear that we may have here a partial basis for a true science of values, and consequently of ethics, social relations, politics, religion, etc."

• • •

"A priori considerations encourage the hypothesis that this superiority in the perception of reality eventuates in a superior ability to reason, to perceive the truth, to come to conclusions, to be logical and to be cognitively efficient, in general."

Motivation And Personality

In the same book, Maslow has used the term, "the self-actualizing person," to designate the rare individual who has achieved that quality of *being* which we might describe as psychologically mature, enlightened and responsible. In his list of characteristics of such people, he makes the striking statement, "None of them is chronically unsure about the difference between right and wrong in his actual living." (p. 220) This statement is particularly noteworthy in view of the widespread confusion, real or contrived, on the issue of right and wrong.

Fritz Kunkel, a psychotherapist who wrote many popular books on psychological subjects, once said in a lecture that when an outer stimulus calling for response really "gets through" to a person's true center (which in this book we have called his *essential self*), his response has the triple character of *courage, understanding,* and *love.*

In a bulletin of the Menninger Foundation, William C. Menninger, M.D. offered the following:

"THE CRITERIA OF EMOTIONAL MATURITY:
HAVING the ability to deal constructively with reality.
HAVING the capacity to adapt to change.
HAVING a relative freedom from symptoms that are produced by tensions and anxieties.

HAVING the capacity to find more satisfaction in giving than receiving.
HAVING the capacity to relate to other people in a consistent manner with mutual satisfaction and helpfulness.
HAVING the capacity to sublimate, to direct one's instinctive hostile energy into creative and constructive outlets.
HAVING the capacity to love."

Menninger Foundation
Bulletin

In *The Art of Loving,* Erich Fromm says:

"To analyze the nature of love is to discover its general absence today and to criticize the social conditions which are responsible for this absence. To have faith in the possibility of love as a social and not only exceptional-individual phenomenon, is a rational faith based on the insight into the very nature of man."

The Art of Loving

The anthropologist, Ashley Montagu, has a number of challenging statements in his book, *On Being Human.* Here are several:

"It is a discovery of the greatest possible significance for mankind that the ethical conception of love independently arrived at by almost all existing peoples is no mere creation of man but is grounded in the biological structure of man as a functioning organism."

• • •

"To love thy neighbor as thyself is not simply good text material for Sunday morning sermons but perfectly sound biology."

• • •

"Man is born for cooperation, not for competition or conflict. This is a basic discovery of modern science. It confirms a discovery made some two thousand years ago by one Jesus of Nazareth. In a word: it is the principle of love which embraces all mankind. It is the principle of humanity, of one world, one brotherhood of peoples."

On Being Human

Pitirim A. Sorokin, noted sociologist who established and directed the Harvard Research Center in Creative Altruism, made the following statement:

> "Now more than ever before I believe in the following truths, which are fully confirmed by our experimental studies:
>
> Hate begets hate, violence engenders violence, hypocrisy is answered by hypocrisy, war generates war, and love creates love.
>
> Unselfish love has enormous creative and therapeutic potentialities, far greater than most people think,
>
> Love is a life-giving force, necessary for physical, mental and moral health.
>
> Altruistic persons live longer than egotistic individuals.
>
> Children deprived of love tend to become vitally, morally, and socially defective.
>
> Love is the most powerful antidote against criminal, morbid, and suicidal tendencies; against hate, fear and psychoneuroses.
>
> It is an indispensable condition for deep and lasting happiness.
>
> It is goodness and freedom at their loftiest.
>
> It is the finest and most powerful educational force for the ennoblement of humanity."
>
> *The Ways and Power of Love*

Recommended Reading

Extended study of the thinking and experience of the authors quoted above can prove rewarding and enriching.

We recommend that you begin with the little book of Ashley Montagu, *On Being Human.* William Glasser's *Reality Therapy* would be an excellent next step.

Mowrer's two books, cited above, and Maslow's *Toward A Psychology of Being* are available in paperback editions. Deeper contact with the thinking of these two men is recommended.

Erich Fromm has written many valuable books but the two cited above (*Man For Himself* and *The Art of Loving*) are good introductions to his insights.

APPENDIX C:
Supplement to Chapter II

Few of us can be fully conscious of the extent, depth and ramifications of the crisis that now confronts our world. But some perspective of its magnitude and character is essential if we are to do our part toward its solution. This appendix is intended to help with that perspective. Some of the symptoms are in the following list of threats to our survival

1. The mounting rate of violent crimes—murder, rape, armed robbery, kidnapping, etc.
2. The frightening growth in terrorism throughout the world.
3. The increasing proliferation of nuclear power plants throughout the world with the resultant radioactive wastes and bomb-producing capabilities that threaten all future generations.
4. The similar threat from the steady build-up of the stock of nuclear weapons. (The present American stock pile adds up to the equivalent of more than ten tons of TNT for every man, woman, and child on the planet. Russia is reported to have an equivalent stock pile.)
5. Explosive racial tensions.
6. The potential of the escalation of the Israeli-Arab or other tensions into World War III, which could end everything we consider worthwhile in life.
7. The present and growing fact of hunger, famine and starvation for millions of the world's population.
8. The threat to our survival by world overpopulation.
9. The pollution and poisoning of the air, water and soil on which our life depends.
10. The threat of world-wide economic collapse.
11. The unbearable, economic cost and waste through our military expenditures and from

the results of our recent Southeast Asian adventure.

12. The greed and graft in high places in government, business, and labor.
13. The breakdown of moral, ethical and spiritual values resulting in such outcomes as the break-up of the family as a basic social institution, the aberrational exploitation of sexual expressions, juvenile delinquency, drug abuse, alcoholism, pornography.
14. Widespread mental illness with its tremendous social and economic cost.
15. The waste and exhaustion of non-renewable natural resources necessary to our way of life.
16. The energy crisis.
17. Widespread unemployment.
18. The inequitable distribution of wealth. ("The rich get richer, the poor get poorer." The statistics support this familiar statement.)
19. The threat to freedom by the continued extreme approaches of communism and fascism in their various forms, including invasions of privacy by bureaucratic wire-tapping and other police-state expressions.
20. The apathy, ignorance and irresponsibility of people relative to their own well-being and that of the planet.
21. The aberrational indoctrination of our children through television.
22. The high social cost of highway accidents.
23. The growth of cynical attitudes toward life and man's future.
24. The threat of general despair and the loss of hope.

Most people have a feeling of impotence when facing the implications of such a list of problems to be solved. The tendency is to feel that their correction must come through legislation and other governmental action. Government, the political aspect of society, is an essential element in the functioning of any group of people. It is that which provides the necessary system and order without which chaos prevails. But we have recently been deeply shocked by the extent to which there has been betrayal of our trust by people we have elected to carry out the functions of government. Personal bad conduct, bribery, overwhelming ambition and greed have existed to an extent we have been reluctant to believe. It is revealing to learn how far officials, elected or appointed to look after the interests of the public, have violated their responsibilities by yielding to the pressures of economically powerful lobbies, motivated by greed and narrow selfish interest. The people of the United States seemed for a time to be in a healthy state of shock, but there is a constant danger of getting accustomed to such a situation, adjusting to it, and therefore doing nothing about it.

In one costly and dangerous aspect of the corrupting influence of selfish economic interests, we have fallen into the trap against which President Eisenhower warned. We are being too greatly controlled by the military-industrial complex which is basically motivated by greed, and not by genuine concern for the nation and its people. Because of the power of that complex we have been drawn into such hopelessly doomed, and economically suicidal, projects as the tragic Southeast Asia effort to "contain Communism" by armed might.

The Pentagon and its allied interests are allowed to waste billions of the nation's dollars in numberless ways. Some of the waste has been by expensive development of already obsolete "defensive" weaponry, some by further expansion of an excessive capacity for "overkill". Much is through innumerable wasteful ways by which the military establishment squanders the money Congress is persuaded to appropriate in the name of "defense". The list is long. All of this we permit because of an artificially stimulated "fear of the Russians." If we do not soon reverse the process, the financial and moral bankruptcy to which all of this is leading, is precisely what the cynics in the Kremlin fervently desire. Are we going to be more stupid than those cynics, who have boasted that they intend to "bury us?" By continuing our present course, we will do most of that job for them!

The American people are generally frightened, as well they may be, by the threat of Communism. Many are also fearful of the danger of Fascism. If either of these totalitarian systems were to get control of our country, that would mark the end of the liberty we so greatly treasure. The concern is well founded. Our practical error lies in the means by which we have sought to prevent the spread of Communism. It has been called "containing Communism." But the longer we use the wrong means, the more real becomes the danger we fear. This is a crucial example of the ignorance of reality to which we have continuously referred.

We have also been led to believe that untrammeled "free enterprise," without any governmental "interference," is an essential element of freedom. The most powerful propaganda for that view is promulgated by vast interrelated economic conglomerates and multinational corporations. By their increasingly monopolistic control of the economy, these powerful groups are themselves rapidly destroying all free enterprise, except their own! They talk free enterprise but their actions deny it. They are not farsighted and wise enough to see that the course they are pursuing is precisely what creates the kind of situation within which communistic take-overs can occur, because by that course the rich continue to get richer, and the poor poorer, until the whole thing explodes. This results from the concentration of dangerous economic power in a group motivated by greed, and having too limited and narrow an understanding of its long range consequences.

Robert McNamara, as President of the World Bank, warned of inevitable world-wide violence and upheaval unless global poverty is reduced. Anyone who can read the signs of the times must recognize the validity of his observation. That kind of violence, upheaval and disorder provide exactly the situation made to order for the communist world plan. When things get so bad for large numbers of people that they feel the situation can't get any worse, they are ready to try

anything that they are told will give them relief from their misery. The situation is then ripe for revolution. When that occurs, totalitarian power is seized by those who are sufficiently powerful and organized to take control. Such a group could be either fascist or communist in its ideology. In Russia, the Bolshevists were sufficiently well organized and ruthless to wrest control from the provisional Kerenski government. Once such totalitarians get control, with concentrated power and the determination to exercise it, it is next to impossible to overturn their regime. The lessons of recent and current history should educate us on that subject if we are open to learn. The American concern, that neither a communist nor a fascist coup shall take place here, is a realistic concern—particularly as our economic stability is under severe strain.

President Hoover pointed out—as have many others—that inner decay, rather than conquest from without, is the way by which a nation loses its destiny. History abundantly demonstrates this. It is to be noted that no one can class either Eisenhower, or Hoover, or McNamara as a "dangerous radical," or as an opponent of free enterprise. We need to pay heed to their perceptive observations.

The headlong rush of revolutionary technology since the dawn of this twentieth century has projected mankind into an entirely new age of human experience. It is like nothing that has ever gone before. At the turn of the century the Wright brothers had not yet made the first airplane flight. It took days, weeks, or months to get from one place on the globe to another. No one had set foot on either the north or south pole and to talk of going there seemed sheer fantasy. Today the point farthest from us on this earth can be reached in hours. Men from the United States have taken a half-million-mile round trip into outer space with a stop-over on the surface of the moon!

At the turn of the century, the telephone would work over only relatively short distances, and Marconi was experimenting with crude wireless telegraph apparatus. Today by radio and television, with the aid of satellites in space, we can be in almost instant communication with the entire globe. We carried on conversations over a distance of a quarter of a million miles with men who had landed on the moon, and have had color photographs transmitted back to us from the surface of Planet Mars, millions of miles away. Truly space has shrunk, and all parts of our planet have become intimately interrelated by these revolutionary factors of speedy travel and instant communication. They have given us means for increasingly effective positive action for the benefit of all mankind.

But, since the turn of the century we have been involved in two world wars. With the discovery of ways to release the energy of the atom, our destructive power has grown fantastically. We now have the ability to make the entire planet uninhabitable and to destroy all mankind. The sobering responsibility which this power imposes upon us is inescapable. However, its magnitude is so terrible that we are constantly tempted to try to ignore it instead of seeking practical ways of controlling it.

The destruction of the Japanese city of Hiroshima by an atomic bomb marked a turning point in human history. Some expressions of concern at that time are worth reviewing. Six months *before* Hiroshima, the February 1945 issue of the *Scientific Monthly*—journal of the American Association for the Advancement of Science—carried this poem:

DOMINION

Now Man must take unto himself dominion,
The sovereignty he has given his inventions.
His is the brain behind his own machinery.
Should ever the lesser dispossess the greater?
The use beneficent, not the use injurious,
Should be his program, his unceasing doctrine.
The silver bird that spreads its wings to heaven
Man's glorious conquest of the sky announces,
But how does Man reward his own bright genius?
By hurling down—upon himself!—destruction.
And on he goes, discovering and inventing,
An artless child near gas with matches playing.
The power he takes from earth's entrails will seize him,
With earth-shaking fury rend him, him and his
offspring.
Before he further searches out the atom,
Let him ask himself this question: "Am I ready?"

Until he is, he had better stay his power
And look within. And look within. God help him!

Elizabeth Parkhill Jordan

The same journal in the issue of October 1946 carried another poem:

ATOMIC POWER

Before recorded history began
Prometheus, symbol of Science, brought us fire,
The altar and the hearth were our desire;
On these were built the faith and hope of man.
Then wood and stone and bronze and steel and steam
In turn became the servants of our will;
Knowledge we got and with it thought to fill

Each need and want, to realize each dream.
Again Prometheus brings a magic gift,
Which scarce we know if we should ban or bless.
The boldest hesitate, the fearful cower,
Before this weapon, deadly, sure and swift.
Amazed we stand, appalled at our success;
For who are we to wield this cosmic power?

Thomson King

At the end of World War II, in his speech accepting the Japanese surrender in Tokyo Harbor, General Douglas MacArthur made a significant statement:

"Men since the beginning of time have sought peace. Various methods through the ages have attempted to devise an international process to prevent or settle disputes between nations. From the very start, workable methods were found insofar as individual citizens were concerned, but the mechanics of an instrumentality of larger international scope have never been successful. Military alliance, balances of power, leagues of nations all in turn failed, leaving the only path to be by way of the crucible of war. The utter destructiveness of war now blots out this alternative. We have had our last chance. If we do not now devise some greater and more equitable system, Armageddon will be at our door. The problem basically is theological and involves a spiritual recrudescence and improvement of human character that will synchro-

> nize with our almost matchless advance in science, art, literature and all material and cultural developments of the last two thousand years. It must be of the spirit if we are to save the flesh."

The succinct observation of another military man, the highly respected General Omar Bradly, is relevant.

> "Our knowledge of science has outstripped our capacity to control it. The world has achieved brilliance without wisdom, power without conscience. Ours is a world of nuclear giants and ethical infants."

After the atomic bombing of Hiroshima and Nagaski, Norman Cousins published a noted editorial, later issued as a book, with the arresting title, *Modern Man Is Obsolete.* In it he spelled out the need for a new humanity and a new responsibility.

Albert Einstein had instigated the research in nuclear fission leading to the atomic bomb, by pointing out its importance to President Roosevelt. After the war, he sought funds for educating the public on the dangers and the responsibility which ensued. In that effort he sent to a number of people telegrams in which he said:

> "OUR WORLD FACES CRISIS AS YET UNPERCEIVED BY THOSE POSSESSING POWER TO MAKE GREAT DECISIONS FOR GOOD OR EVIL. THE UNLEASHED POWER OF THE ATOM HAS CHANGED EVERYTHING SAVE OUR MODES OF THINKING AND WE THUS DRIFT TOWARD UNPARALLELED CATASTROPHE."

Some months after Hiroshima, Hermann Hagedorn wrote and published a striking epic poem, *The Bomb That Fell on America.* Its theme, movingly and dramatically presented was: "135 million Americans have to grow up overnight."

Additional perspective can be obtained by reading one or more of a number of readily available books. Any of the following can provide a good beginning:

William H. Boyer, *Alternative Futures: Designing Social Change*

Barry Commoner, *The Closing Circle*
Barry Commoner, *The Poverty of Power*
Alvin Toffler, *The Eco-spasm Report*
Paul R. Ehrlich, *The End of Affluence*
Paul R. Ehrlich, *The Population Bomb*
E. F. Schumacher, *Small is Beautiful: Economics As If People Mattered*
Meadows, et al., *The Limits To Growth*
Mesarovic, Mihajlo, and Edward Pestel, *Mankind At The Turning Point*
Garrett de Bell, Ed., *The Environmental Handbook*
Frances Moore Lappe, *Diet For a Small Planet*
Barbara Ward, *Spaceship Earth*
Erich Fromm, *The Revolution of Hope*

A pair of books well worthy of attention for the insight they provide on the methods of the two authoritarian and totalitarian political ideologies, Communism and Fascism, were written by Harry and Bonaro Overstreet: *What We Must Know About Communism,* and *The Strange Tactics of Extremism.*

APPENDIX D:
Supplement to Chapter III

Sample Manifestations of the Existential Self

"In its 200th year the Republic is suffering middle-age spread. We the people are at least a billion pounds overweight, which is not surprising considering the calorie content of the nation's favorite drugs, alcoholic beverages. Last year Americans swallowed *621 million gallons of wine and distilled spirits,* and the equivalent of *49 billion 12-ounce bottles of beer.* With all that sloshing through its system, the populace probably would be short of breath even if it had not smoked *8.7 billion cigars* and *nearly 600 billion cigarettes.* Yankee Doodle, keep it up, if you don't care a fig about longevity."

"The principal killers of Americans are heart disease, stroke and cancer, all of which are often closely related to victims' habits. Fifty-five per cent of all deaths involve diseases of the heart and blood vessels, diseases frequently associated with obesity and lack of exercise. According to National Cancer Institute statistics, 70,000 of the 80,000 lung-cancer deaths each year result from smoking. Women and teen-agers are smoking more, and the lung-cancer death rate among women has tripled in the last fourteen years. It soon may equal the rate among men. As the cigarette company says, congratulations: you've come a long way, Baby." (Emphasis Added)

George F. Will
Newsweek, April 19, 1976

Self-imposed Obstacles to Perception

"Nothing is easier than self-deceit. For what each man wishes, that he also believes to be true."

Demosthenes
4th Century B.C.

"Science is the only way we have of shoving truth down the reluctant throat."

A. H. Maslow

"One may be deceived in many ways; one may be deceived by believing the false, but one may also be deceived by not believing the true; one may be deceived by appearances, but one may also be deceived by the appearance of shrewdness, by the flattering conceit which is absolutely certain it cannot be deceived."

Søren Kierkegaard
Works of Love

"Let us think over the situation. We can see what the human mind is doing. It is acting on an innate impulse to reject anything strange; for that which does not fit easily into the familiar world seems to it fantastic and bizarre."

G. N. M. Tyrrell
The Nature of Human Personality

"It is frequently the tragedy of the great artist, as it is of the great scientist, that he frightens the ordinary man. If he is more than a popular story-teller it may take humanity a generation to absorb and grow accustomed to the new geography with which the scientist or artist presents us. Even then, perhaps only the more imaginative and literate may accept him. Subconsciously the genius is feared as an image breaker; frequently he does not accept the opinions of the mass, or man's opinion of himself. He has voiced through the ages, in one form or another, this very loneliness and detachment which Dewey saw so clearly as the outcome of our extending knowledge. The custom-bound, uneducated, intolerant man projects his fear and hatred upon the seer. The artist is frequently a human mirror. If what we see there displeases us, if we see all too clearly our own insignificance and vanity, we tend to revolt, not against ourselves, but in order to martyrize the unfortunate soul who forced us into self-examination."

Loren Eiseley
The Night Country

The Civilizing Process

"Civilization, a much abused word, stands for a high matter quite apart from telephones and electric lights. It is a matter of imponderables, of delight in the things of the mind, of love of beauty, of honor, grace, courtesy, delicate feeling. Where imponderables are the things of first importance, there is the height of civilization, and if, at the same time, the power to act exists unimpaired, human life has reached a level seldom attained and very seldom surpassed. Few individuals are capable of the achievement; periods of history which have produced such men in sufficient numbers to stamp their age are rare indeed.

Edith Hamilton
The Greek Way To Western Civilization

". . . there is the fact, which John Dewey has pointed out, that wisdom is not an intellectual term. It does not denote profound, systematic knowledge of the ultimate pattern of things, but an active preference for the best ends and means of life. It is loyalty to the better values, to the goods which are satisfying in the light of reflection; and it implies active interest in bringing those goods into more general and secure enjoyment."

Max C. Otto
Science And The Moral Life

". . . the concept of the whole man is not adequate as an aim of education. . . . The complete man must be a good man. Moral character arises from the molding of the native powers to ideal aims. The final secular good is the dedication of the self to an ideal higher than the self—the devotion to truth and to one's neighbor."

The Harvard Committee
General Education in a Free Society.

"Man is still young on the face of the earth; civilization is still in its infancy. *Homo sapiens* has not yet realized his strength and his greatness; nor does he see, except dimly, the heights to which civilization can reach."

George Gallup
The Miracle Ahead

Signs of Hope

"The religious renewal we see happening about us—especially among disaffiliated young people, but by no means only among them—seems to me neither trivial nor irresponsible, neither uncivil nor indecent. On the contrary, I accept it as a profoundly serious sign of the times, a necessary phase of our cultural evolution, and—potentially—a life-enhancing influence of incalculable value. I believe it means we have arrived, after long journeying, at an historical vantage point from which we can at last see where the wasteland ends and where a culture of human wholeness and fulfillment begins. We can now recognize that the fate of the soul is the fate of the social order; that if the spirit within us withers so too will all the world we build about us. Literally so. What, after all, is the ecological crisis that now captures so much belated attention but the inevitable extroversion of a blighted psyche? Like inside, like outside. In the eleventh hour, the very physical environment suddenly looms up before us as the outward mirror of our inner condition, for many the first discernible symptom of advanced disease within.

Theodore Roszak
Where The Wasteland Ends

The Principle of Detachment

"*The true value of a human being* is determined primarily by the measure and the sense in which he has attained to liberation from the self."

Albert Einstein
The World as I See It

"The only kind of liberty which is workable in the real world is the liberty of the disinterested man, of the man who has transformed his passions by an understanding of necessity. He can, as Confucius said, follow what his heart desires without transgressing what is right. For he has learned to desire what is right."

Walter Lippman
A Preface to Morals

". . . The only possible virtue in being a civilized man instead of a barbarian, an ignoramus, or a moron is in being a free, responsible individual with a mind of one's own."

Herbert J. Muller
The Uses of The Past

"Fully adult minds . . . have met and made peace with reality. They have not only reclaimed the creative imagination of childhood, but have married it to understanding and have chastened it with reality. Such minds are free. In the later decades of life they grow to a power and a delight which may altogether transcend the more physically conditioned ecstacies of youth . . . having had the courage to grow up, they become the true giants of the earth."

William H. Sheldon
Psychology And The Promethean Will

"At this point it becomes necessary to say something about that ideal individual into whom the changers of heart desire to transform themselves and others. Every age and class has had its ideal. The ruling classes in Greece idealized the magnanimous man, a sort of scholar-and-gentleman. Kshatriyas in early India and feudal nobles in mediaeval Europe held up the ideal of the chivalrous man. The *honnete homme* makes his appearance as the ideal of seventeenth-century gentlemen; the *philosophe,* as the ideal of their descendants in the eighteenth century. The nineteenth century idealized the respectable man. The twentieth has already witnessed the rise and fall of the liberal man and the emergence of the sheep-like social man and the god-like Leader. Meanwhile the poor and downtrodden have always dreamed nostalgically of a man ideally well-fed, free, happy, and unoppressed.

"Among this bewildering multiplicity of ideals which shall we choose? The answer is that we shall choose none. For it is clear that each one of these contradictory ideals is the fruit of particular social circumstances. To some extent, of course, this is true of every thought and aspiration that has ever been formulated. Some thoughts and aspirations, however, are manifestly less dependent on particular social circumstances than others. And here a significant fact emerges: all the ideals of human behaviour formulated by those who have been most successful in freeing themselves from the prejudices of their time and place are singularly alike. Liberation from prevailing conventions of thought, feeling and behaviour is accomplished most effectively by the practice of disinterested virtues and through direct insight into the real nature of ultimate reality. (Such insight is a gift, inherent in the individual; but, though inherent, it cannot manifest itself completely except where certain conditions are fulfilled. The principal precondition of insight is, precisely, the practice of disinterested virtues.) To some extent critical intellect is also a liberating force. But the way in which intellect is used depends upon the will. Where the will is not disinterested, the intellect tends to be used (outside the non-human fields of technology, science or pure mathematics) merely as an instrument for the rationalization of passion and prejudice, the justification of self-interest. That is why so few even of the acutest philosophers have succeeded in liberating themselves completely from the narrow prison of their age and country. It is seldom indeed that they achieve as much freedom as the mystics and the founders of religion. The most nearly free men have always been those who combined virtue with insight.

"Now, among these freest of human beings there has been, for the last eighty or ninety generations, substantial agreement in regard to the ideal individual. The enslaved have held up for admiration now this model of a man, now that; but at all times and in all places, the free have spoken with only one voice.

"It is difficult to find a single word that will adequately describe the ideal man of the free philosophers and the founders of religions. "Non-attached" is perhaps the best. The ideal man is the non-attached man. Non-attached to his bodily sensations and lusts. Non-attached to his craving for power and possessions. Non-attached to the objects of these various desires. Non-attached to his anger and hatred; non-attached to his exclusive loves. Non-attached to wealth, fame, social position. Non-attached even to science, art, speculation, philanthropy. Yes, non-attached even to these. For, like patriotism, in Nurse Cavell's phrase, "they are not enough." Non-attachment to self and to what are called "the things of this world" has always been associated in the teachings of the philosophers and the founders of religions with attachment to an ultimate reality greater and more significant than the self. Greater and more significant than even the best things that this world has to offer. Of the nature of this ultimate reality I shall speak in the last chapters of this book. All that I need do in this place is to point out that the ethic of non-attachment has always been correlated with cosmologies that affirm the existence of a spiritual reality underlying the phenomenal world and imparting to it whatever value or significance it possesses."

Aldous Huxley
Ends And Means

APPENDIX E
Supplement to Chapter IV

Some significant words on the subject of wisdom are contained in an eloquent tribute by one great American judge, Learned Hand, to another, Benjamin Nathan Cardozo:

> "And what is wisdom—that gift of God which the great prophets of his race exalted? I do not know; like you, I know it when I see it, but I cannot tell of what it is composed.
>
> "One ingredient I think I do know: the wise man is the detached man. By that I mean more than detached from his grosser interests, his advancement, and his gain.
>
> "Many of us can be that—I dare to believe that most judges can be, and are. I am thinking of something far more subtly interfused. Our convictions, our outlook, the whole make-up of our thinking, which we cannot help bringing to the decision of every question, is the creature of our past; and into our past have been woven all sorts of opportunities lost through cowardice, of frustrated ambitions with their envies, and of hopes of preferment with their corruptions, which, long since forgotten, still determine our conclusions.
>
> "A wise man is usually exempt from the handicap of such a past; he is a runner stripped for the race; he can weigh the conflicting factors of his problem without always finding himself in one scale or the other.
>
> "Cardozo was such a man; his gentle nature had in it no acquisitiveness; he did not use himself as a measure of value; the secret of his humor—a precious gift that he did not wear upon his sleeve—lay in his ability to get outside of himself, and look back.
>
> "Yet from this self-effacement came a power greater than the power of him who ruleth a city. He was wise because his spirit was uncontaminated, because he knew no violence, or hatred, or envy, or jealousy, or ill-will. I believe that it was this purity that chiefly made him the judge we so much revere; more than his learning, his acuteness, and his fabulous industry.
>
> ". . . In this America of ours where the passion for publicity is a disease, and where swarms of foolish, tawdry moths dash with rapture into its consuming fire, it was a rare good fortune that brought to such eminence a man so reserved, so unassuming, so retiring, so gracious to high and low, and so serene. He is

gone, and while the west is still lighted with his radiance, it is well for us to pause and take account of our own coarser selves. He has a lesson to teach us if we care to stop and learn; a lesson quite at variance with most that we practice, and much that we profess."

The Spirit of Liberty
Papers and addresses of Learned Hand

A professor of the philosophy of religion, Henry Nelson Wieman, pointed out important distinctions in meaning among the terms: *belief, knowledge,* and *faith.* His analysis can be helpful.

"Belief is holding any proposition to be true. Knowledge is accepting a proposition to be true on grounds of good evidence. Faith is accepting a belief in such a way that it transforms one's way of living. A belief becomes knowledge when it is supported by good evidence. It becomes a faith when it shapes the controlling loyalties of a life. Knowledge is not necessarily faith. A man might know many things which do not appreciably modify the directional thrusts of his life. On the other hand, however, a belief which does do this, and hence is a faith, might have as much evidence to support it as any case of knowledge, and hence would be knowledge as well as being faith. It is the life-transforming power of the belief, and not the lack of good evidence, which makes it a faith. To be sure, beliefs which do determine a man's way of life, and hence are his faith, may lack evidence. But there are no beliefs which should be kept more strictly within the bounds of solid knowledge than those which give direction to the total movement of a man's life; for if they are false the evil is very great. On the other hand, beliefs which do not make or destroy a personality can be false without so much disaster. Therefore a faith, more than any other kind of belief, should be knowledge in the sense of being based on good evidence."

The Growth of Religion

Recommended Reading

There is a vast collection of books on prayer, meditation, and mysticism. To begin investigation of this body of literature a good start can be made with John B. Magee's book, *Reality and Prayer* (initially published by Harper's in 1957 and now available in paperback).

Gerald Heard has provided a valuable introduction in *A Preface to Prayer* (published by Harper's in 1944). His pamphlets, *Training For The Life of The Spirit*, have been republished in paperback edition, (East Ridge Press, 1975).

The classic work on mysticism is Evelyn Underhill's scholarly work first published in 1910, entitled simply, *Mysticism.* This has gone through many editions and is now available in paperback. She has also written a number of shorter works on mysticism and various aspects of the religious life.

APPENDIX F:

Supplement to Chapter V

A natural historical prejudice prevails among Jews against anything having to do with Jesus, because of what the Jewish people have suffered at the hands of Christians, who profess to be followers of Jesus. Of particular interest, therefore, are favorable Jewish evaluations of Jesus. One such is contained in a book by a Jewish scholar who, for over twenty years, was head of the Department of Education and Psychology at the Carnegie Institute of Technology. He wrote:

> "Jesus offended the good Jews of his day, and he would likewise offend the good Christians of today were he to appear in their midst with the message he brought to his contemporaries. The Jew forgets, because of what the Christian has done to him in the name of Jesus, that Jesus was a genius of the spirit, and the Christian ignores, because of what he claims the Jew did to Jesus, that Jesus was a Jew. Between the two warring camps the great Galilean is maligned by one and distorted by the other; between them the supreme religious mind of the ages "has nowhere to lay his head." But Jesus the Jew and genius lives on, and will continue to live on, as a reproach and a promise to his detractors and distorters: a reproach to their blindness and a promise for their enlightenment."
>
> Max Schoen
> *The Man Jesus Was*

Many of the quotations attributed to Jesus in this book are taken from *Jesus as Teacher* by Henry Burton Sharman. This is a product of the kind of critical, scholarly work to which reference has been made. Sharman's work has made a significant contribution toward reclaiming the historical Jesus from the nineteen centuries of tradition by which he has been obscured. Much of Sharman's original work is contained in his doctoral thesis: *The Teaching of Jesus About The Future* (The University of Chicago Press, 1909) and in *Son of Man And Kingdom of God: A Critical Study* (Harper & Brothers, 1943). *Jesus As Teacher,* originally published by Harper's in 1935, has been reissued by Sequoia Seminar Foundation.

Some additional perspective on the historical Jesus is provided by Leroy Waterman in *The Religion of*

Jesus (Harper & Brothers, 1952) and also in the same writer's *Religion Faces The World Crisis* (previously cited).

In seminars offered by Creative Initiative Foundation and by Sequoia Seminar Foundation, opportunities are provided for further study of the life and teaching of Jesus, and their relevance for today.

APPENDIX G:
Supplement to Chapter VI

Recommended Reading

For those desiring supplementary reading on the role of women, one good starting point is M. Esther Harding, M.D., *The Way of All Women*, Longmans, Green & Co., 1932. Another is Irene Claremont de Castillejo, *Knowing Woman, A Feminine Psychology.* Harper Colophon Books. Harper & Row, Publishers. An illuminating collection of writings on women's struggle for equal recognition is assembled in *Masculine/Feminine: Readings in Sexual Mythology and the Liberation of Women*, Edited by Betty Roszak and Theodore Roszak. Harper Colophon Books. Harper & Row, Publishers.

On the stages of psychological growth, a comprehensive and helpful survey of the life from birth to death is in Theodore Lidz, *The Person.* Basic Books, Inc., Publishers. Another authoritative book on the subject is Erik H. Erikson, *Childhood and Society,* W. W. Norton.

All of the illustrations in this book were created and prepared by a group of people under the direction of Mike Lee.
Production and composition by Holmes Composition Service, San Jose, California.
Printing and binding by Banta West, Sparks, Nevada.
Cover printing by Peninsula Press, Mountain View, California.

Our world has come up against the most severe crisis mankind has ever faced. The issue is survival. The crisis is the result of man's *ignorance*—ignorance of his true nature and destiny, ignorance of his proper relationship to the world which produced him, and ignorance of the attitude and action he must take and the process he must undergo for his own survival and self realization. This book outlines the principles which govern that process.

The Creative Initiative Foundation is a non-profit educational foundation which exists to help people find and embark upon the way to personal and global fulfillment. It offers courses and seminars in which people can work in cooperative groups toward both the realization of the high potential which is their inheritance, and the solution of the "environmental" crisis that confronts us.

The main center for the weekend and five-day Creative Initiative seminars is in a secluded and beautiful setting among the redwoods in the Santa Cruz Mountains of California. There are other seminar centers in the states of Washington, Oregon, Colorado, and Virginia. Study groups are carried on in an increasing number of additional states. An introductory course, called *Challenge To Change,* is generally conducted in small groups of ten to a dozen people, meeting in the living rooms of the participants.

Information regarding the on-going Creative Initiative educational program may be obtained by writing to Creative Initiative Foundation, 222 High Street, Palo Alto, California 94301.